Quick-Sttartt Guide

So you're ready and eager to start but don't know where to begin? I've got you covered! Here's a quick-start guide to give you the most important information first before moving on to the rest of the nitty-gritty feeding details, tools, and tips you'll need.

There are three key things you should know once you get approval from either your pediatrician or dietitian that you can begin solids:

First: Understand the important safety and choking information <u>here</u>. Find out with regards to stifling dangers, the contrast among choking and gagging, and how to deal with a baby that is showing stifling conduct during supper time. But don't let these deter you from trying the baby-led weaning (BLW) method.

Second: Is there any family history of food allergies? If the answer is no, then you don't have to worry about limiting food when you start BLW, with the exception of foods that are normally advised against for young infants, such as highly processed foods, salt, cow's milk as a primary drink, and honey. If the answer is yes, then you have to be more careful and may need to avoid or delay introducing foods that are known to be common allergens. Review pages 8 and 9 for more information about allergies and foods to avoid.

Third: Is your baby developmentally ready? Go <u>here</u> to review the key developmental stages for food readiness and answer the questions to determine if your baby is ready.

Once you've reviewed these key parameters and have determined that baby is developmentally ready for solids, then you can start BLW. I recommend starting with <u>Roasted Sweet Potato Sticks, Steamed Broccoli with Orange Zest, and Egg and Avocado Crepe. These are all super easy, require minimal prep and cooking time (no more than 35 minutes per recipe), and are doable for a first-time parent or caregiver, whether you have cooking experience or not.</u>

CH1

CH1

Baby-Led Weaning, tthe Easy Way

Introducing solid foods to your baby is a major milestone, and baby-led weaning (BLW) is a wonderful way to engage with your baby as they discover a whole new world of flavors and textures. I understand that you might still have questions or be a little nervous. That's why, in this chapter, I will explain BLW, tell you what to look out for, and describe the tools you will need to make your experience as easy, fun, and stress-free as possible.

What Is BLW?

BLW is a taking care of strategy initially presented by a general wellbeing medical attendant named Gill Rapley in 2005. It is an elective way to deal with utilizing customary coddled purees that permits a baby to self-feed beginning at 6 years old months.

During the initial a half year of life, newborn children exclusively depend on bosom milk or recipe for their sustenance. At the point when they are formatively prepared, they can be methodiclly acquainted with strong food sources. As their admission of solids gradually expands, the bosom milk or equation is steadily removed, consequently weaning the child from bosom milk or formula.

The food starting period is a critical stage in a baby's life; it shapes their food inclinations and eating conduct in youth, which thus impact their relationship with food during puberty and adulthood. Eventually, BLW is a simple

method for presenting strong food that can have extraordinary advantages down the road.

Little Steps, Big Benefits

This is the place where the pleasant starts helping your little one to partake in the food that you appreciate as a family. Assuming you slip into it and try to serve your child age-and surface suitable food sources, you'll before long be partaking in the many advantages of BLW, including the following:

→ **Ease: In correlation with making child purees at home, BLW is a lot more straightforward.** Child can eat with you, you don't need to totally overlook your feast while you feed them, and you don't need to think about when they're eager or full.

→ **Flavor openness:** BLW is a strategy that energizes the

investigation of an assortment of flavors, including normally sweet (without added sugar), sharp, exquisite, umami, and surprisingly harsh. Furthermore it doesn't stop there; you can likewise try different things with spices and flavors (however not excessively fiery just yet!).

→ **Self-guideline:** BLW shows babies instinctive eating. This implies that a kid eats when they are eager, and they pick what they need to eat, how much, and when to stop in light of their own totality prompts. Instinctive eating assists your child construct a solid and positive relationship with food.

→ **Palate and fastidiousness:** Although there's no proof as of now that BLW can further develop a child's sense of taste and diminish meticulousness, it is accepted that a presentation stage that incorporates a wide assortment of food varieties will decrease the likelihood of particular eating.

→ **Motor and oral abilities:** Self-taking care of offers babies the chance to chip away at their dexterity, getting a handle on and pincer abilities, and gumming and biting capacity consistently. BLW additionally helps cultivate early nonverbal relational abilities as child gives

signals for hunger, needing more, and being done.

→ **Eating with the family:** This is the most awesome aspect yet. With BLW, you don't need to cook separate food varieties for child. All things considered, you can partake in your suppers together.

Food introduction is an experiment and should be fun for both you and baby. This is the time to foster a healthy relationship with food. Allow your baby to learn to enjoy not only the taste but also the smell and the texture of their food. Baby will likely engage with their food in many different ways—and it may get messy. They may get food on their face, in their hair, or up their nose. There may be days when they are more interested in smearing their food on the high-chair tray, or they may even throw food on the ground. If you cringe a bit at the potential mess, imagine watching your baby's facial expressions as they explore and discover new flavors and textures. Remember, play is the way babies learn—and you want them to learn to feed themselves—so relax, take a few pictures, and have fun!

Getting Started with Solids

Once your pediatrician has given you the thumbs up to present solids, you will probably be anxious to make the following stride. It's conceivable that your child has been noticing you eat for some time now and pondering, "When do I get a taste?" You might decide to begin with the customary puree approach or attempt the BLW strategy. Assuming you're experiencing difficulty choosing, have confidence that BLW has been explored and demonstrated to be a protected and successful taking care of strategy for newborn children. A BLISS study (see References) did not find an increased choking hazard with this method when it was carried out cautiously. The magnificence of BLW is it truly isn't muddled as long as your child is formatively prepared. What's more assuming you pick BLW, you may likewise be amazed to find that children can eat obviously superior to we give them credit for.

To get everything rolling with BLW, basically offer food sources that are old enough fitting size and surface for your child. Other than a few important things to avoid during baby's first year (here), most food varieties are permitted as long as there's no huge history of a family sensitivity. In any case, this doesn't mean you just put the food on child's plate and leave. You should sit close to them to guarantee they are biting and gulping securely. The following segment incorporates simple to-adhere to rules to assist you with getting off to a decent beginning with BLW, regardless of whether doing it with your first youngster or your fourth.

Developmental Stages

Generally, child can begin tolerating solids at a half year old enough or changed a half year for preemies (a half year from the child's expected date). Introducing food too early, such as before 4 months old, poses a risk for aspiration, or inhaling food into the airway.

Once child is prepared for solids, focus on their coordinated movements, which can assist you with recognizing which phase of BLW food is generally fitting. Children start with a palmar handle as a baby almost immediately (consider how they get your finger). To this end children start with food sources in strips that they can take hold of with their entire hand. They will then move on to a raking grasp, that is, grabbing things with all of their fingers, around 7 or 8 months (so continuing to cut food into strips is helpful at this stage) and then to pincer grasp starting at around 9 months. Pincer handle permits child to get individual bits of food, so cutting food varieties into little diced pieces is suggested at this stage.

Most children are down for anything introduced to them, making food a fun and simple expansion to the day. It's essential to comprehend that during the beginning phases of strong food presentation, the most common way of investigating flavors and surfaces matters more than the volume drank, since your child's fundamental sustenance is as yet coming from human milk or formula.

Don't feel that you have missed the BLW boat assuming your child began on purees first; it's never past the point where it is possible to begin BLW. That is one of BLW's extraordinary benefits: it's adaptable and flexible so it squeezes into your life at whatever point you need to start.

When Is My Baby Ready?

How can you say whether child is formatively prepared to begin solids? There are a couple of signs to search for. Ensure child has arrived at the accompanying achievements before you begin:

→ **Holding their neck and head up without help.** Ensure that child can hold up their neck and head autonomously, so they can swallow solids without causing desire (food getting breathed in into the lungs).

→ **Sitting up with help.** Child ought to have the option to sit with back and body support, for example, in a high chair.

→ **"Biting" food by moving their gums all over or in a side-to-side movement.** They needn't bother with teeth to have the option to bite; they can gum delicate foods.

→ **Moving food from the front of the tongue to the back and gulping.** In the event that they continue to push the food out with their tongue, they are not exactly ready.

→ **Showing interest in the food you are eating.** Assuming you notice child watching you eat and opening their mouth when a spoon is offered, this is a decent sign they might be ready.

Keeping It Simple

Remember that making food for your baby need not be expensive, hard, complicated, or overwhelming. Whether you are new to cooking or are simply trying to learn which foods to introduce to

child and when, you're perfectly located. You don't need to make a special effort to plan separate food varieties for child. The plans in this book are simple and speedy, will give you and child a fun new action to do together, and can likewise be effortlessly adjusted for more established babies and grown-ups in the family. You can begin with one basic food-one that you like to eat or would like your child to try.

Baby's First Foods

Many of my patients ask what is the best first nourishment for child. The American Academy of Pediatrics (AAP) proposes that the request where you present specific food sources, like oat, natural product, vegetables, dairy, and meat, matters not as much as offering food varieties cautiously and attentively.

The current rules from the AAP prescribe holding up three to five days between presenting new food sources. Nonetheless, assuming there is no critical history of food sensitivity in the family, numerous pediatricians and dietitians (counting myself) recommend offering another food each a couple of days. Arising research recommends that early strong food presentation essentially diminishes the possibilities that a kid will foster a food sensitivity. Refer to the allergen section for more details.

Portions and Nutrition

Between 6 and 7 months old enough, the food you acquaint with child is viewed as correlative taking care of, and that implies that it is a special reward to their standard eating routine of bosom milk or equation. An overall guideline is to take care of your child around 1 tablespoon for each nutrition type each extended period old enough. But try not to worry too much about portion sizes at this time. Keep in mind, they are as yet getting the sustenance they need from human milk or formula.

There are three objectives at this beginning phase: to empower and regard child's natural self-appreciation guideline (let them eat when they are

hungry and stop when they are full), to offer an assortment of flavors and surfaces, and to urge child to contact, smell, lick, and chew their food so they can dominate their oral coordinated movements. The BLW strategy is ideal for achieving these objectives. At the point when you build up this establishment, they will normally advance to eating (biting and gulping) the food varieties being offered.

Cues and Signals

When infants can't yet completely convey in words, parental figures need to give close consideration to the signs and signals they provide for show hunger. They might pucker or lick their lips, cry, become grouchy, or put their clench hand in their mouth.

You can likewise show them straightforward signs. For instance, you can show them the sign language word for *food* (see Resources) while saying the word *food* and then immediately offering them food. Rehash this at each supper to assist them with learning by affiliation. Other supportive signs incorporate those for milk, *more*, and all done, and making an overstated biting movement can urge them to bite and move their gums to crush food.

P IS FOR PUREES, POSSIBLY

Remember that BLW is not the only way to feed baby. It's your choice whether this is the method that you want to pursue or you prefer strictly the puree route. Many people—myself included—choose to combine puree and BLW methods when baby is ready for solids. This can be due to daycare rules or because other caregivers don't feel comfortable with BLW. There's no rule that you must stick to one technique or the other—a combination of both methods is perfectly fine. You can still foster self-feeding with purees, using a preloaded spoon that has a sturdy grip so that baby can improve their skills.

Approaching Allergies, and Foods to Avoid

In investigations distributed in the New England Journal of Medicine and the AAP's Pediatrics (among others), early prologue to food (at around a half year old enough) has been displayed to lessen the likelihood of fostering a food sensitivity. Nonetheless, there are also a few hard rules on the best ways to introduce common allergens safely as well as strict guidelines for avoiding certain allergens completely if your baby is diagnosed during early infancy with food allergies.

This segment will likewise survey what you really want to know about separating among choking and stifling, as most unseasoned parents regularly botch them for the equivalent thing.

Allergen Introductions

Emerging examination gives solid proof showing that early allergen prologue to children has better outcomes in diminishing food sensitivities further down the road. The American Academy of Allergy, Asthma, and Immunology and the AAP Nutrition Committee have additionally recognized the eight most normal food allergens-eggs, cow's milk, fish, shellfish, peanuts, tree nuts, wheat, and soy-can be generally securely presented once the child is formatively prepared, around a half year old enough. Also, these sources show that deferring presentation of these allergens may really expand your child's danger for fostering a food allergy.

If your child is at high danger for a food sensitivity (for instance, a parent or kin has one), it's critical to get a reference to an allergist for testing before presenting any of the main eight allergenic food varieties. On the off chance that there's a generally safe level, you can begin presenting the normal food allergens each in turn, sitting tight for three to five days in between.

It's ideal assuming you can serve the allergen in detachment. In the event that that is unrealistic, you can blend it in with food varieties you definitely know are alright for your child. Since peanuts and nuts are difficult to bite and a gagging peril for children, they are best added as a powder or dissolved nut margarine that can undoubtedly be blended into other safe food sources. Shellfish and fish can be mixed into glue and filled in as a patty or can be meagerly cut or hacked. Eggs can be mixed and made into an omelet and cut into sticks. You can serve cheddar or entire milk yogurt, and tofu, produced using soy, is an incredible fresh start for you to work with.

If your child has a food sensitivity, inside the space of minutes or hours you will see a response, from the advancement of hives to something more serious, like hypersensitivity (inconvenience breathing, wheezing, or shock), which requires prompt clinical attention.

Foods to Avoid (for Now)

Although BLW is an extraordinary method for acquainting your child with a wide assortment of food sources, there are a couple of food sources that you should be cautious with or keep away from altogether.

→ **Cow's milk:** Although cheddar and yogurt are alright, cow's milk (and even plant-based milk) is for the most part not suggested as an essential drink before 1 year old, since it needs many key supplements that infants need, and its high protein content can pressure their kidneys. It tends to be utilized in cooking however ought not supplant recipe or human milk.

→ **Honey:** Children under 1 year old ought not be given honey, incorporating items made with honey, like graham saltines. Honey might contain clostridium microorganisms, which can cause newborn child botulism.

→ **Hard-to-bite food sources:** Hard crude vegetables, entire nuts, and entire dried natural products are generally stifling risks for child. However, if the texture is altered to make them soft and palatable, such as by steaming vegetables or grating them into small soft pieces, or finely grinding nuts, these foods become safe for baby and can be introduced. Finely cleaved dried organic products can be served to children 9 months and older.

→ Processed food sources: Highly handled food sources,
including lunch meat, wieners, ham, frankfurter, and
bacon, are frequently high in fat, sugar, and sodium,
which put pointless weight on little kidneys.

→ Salt: No extra table salt is required while getting
ready nourishment for a baby more youthful than 1
year old.

The 411 on Gagging and Choking

Every parent's or alternately guardian's bad dream is a newborn
child stifling on food. This not exclusively is a horrendous
encounter yet will thwart child's advancement with eating
assuming that it happens every now and again. Subsequently,
it's essential to perceive the indications of stifling and how to
separate them from gagging.

WHAT IS GAGGING?

A child's throat is little at a half year old enough it's 7 to 8 mm
in width, which is about the size of a pea. At 10 months to 7 years,
it's 8 to 11 mm, or ½ inch. Choking is a typical reflex that
happens when infants are first figuring out how to eat. It is a
characteristic defensive component to prevent them from
gagging. For instance, assuming they take a nibble of food that is
too large, they might choke, which can likewise prompt throwing
up or hurling. You need them to figure out how to take a more
modest chomp, bite better, and swallow a more modest piece of
food next time.

WHAT IS CHOKING?

Choking is the point at which a food is totally obstructing a child's
aviation route (windpipe), making them not be able to inhale, talk,
or cry.

What would it be a good idea for you to do when your child is
stifling? Attempt to keep mentally collected. Investigate child's

mouth to check whether you can eliminate any food lumps reachable withoutpushing thefoodfartherin. Another

choice is to turn your child facedown with one of your hands holding their body and supporting the jawline, or spot them facedown on your lap, and utilize the impact point of the other hand to give five back blows between the shoulder bones prior to managing CPR. On the off chance that that is unrealistic, or then again on the off chance that you are not comfortable or sure with baby emergency treatment and CPR, call 911 immediately.

Any food can be a stifling peril, however be particularly wary of food sources that are little, hard, and round, like grapes, cherry tomatoes, entire berries, and nuts or other whole entire food sources. You should cut little grapes in quarters and greater grapes in eight little pieces, guaranteeing each piece is not exactly ½ inch wide in any direction.

T IS FOR TRYING (AND TRYING AGAIN)

Now that you've learned the basics about when to introduce solid foods, there are a couple of insights into infant behavior that you'll need to understand as you begin the process. For example, some babies just won't be into solid foods early on, and some might reject certain flavors. Eating is a learned behavior; consistent exposure and the eating environment are the most important factors during the early stage. Don't give up if your baby doesn't like a food the first time; it may take them up to 10 times or more before they eat it.

Toddler at the Table

Once you have dominated food presentations, taking care of your child into toddlerhood will become simpler and less distressing. One of the advantages of BLW is that your kid figures out how to appreciate food sources that the family eats, and the plans from this book-while fundamentally child centered can be adjusted for and delighted in by the whole family. This is particularly useful assuming you have a more established youngster or your energy is coming up short, since you can simplify changes to the family feast prior to serving it to your child as opposed to making them a whole

separate meal.

As you've learned, BLW directs no particular food varieties to begin with and on second thought underlines assortment. The objective is to permit your child to attempt 100 food varieties when they turn 1, nonetheless don't worry in the event that you can't get to that number. Salt is no longer as large a worry once they are more than a year old. Assuming you are making something hot, eliminate child's part prior to adding the flavor. You might be shocked to learn, however, that a few babies can deal with zest very well.

You ought to likewise begin inviting your baby into the kitchen to find out with regards to the cooking system. Flushing vegetables, blending fixings in a bowl, emptying the substance into a baking container or biscuit tin, and orchestrating vegetables on a sheet search for gold are for the most part instances of how you can include youthful ones in the kitchen.

D IS FOR DIGESTION AND DIAPERS

Let's talk about the big changes that occur on the changing table when you start feeding babies food. What goes in must come out, right? Don't feel worried or shocked when gassiness, constipation, quality, quantity, color, smell, and stool consistency change when new foods, and solid foods in particular, are introduced.

Every baby is different; some have an easier time transitioning than others. If constipation occurs, start giving baby more fruits, such as prunes, pears, and peaches, or a small amount of fruit juice mixed with water (1:1 ratio); just be sure not to offer more than 4 ounces of fruit juice per day. Foods such as blueberries, beets, and avocado can change the color or smell of baby's poop. Also note that certain foods may not get digested well and can come out in pieces, such as corn, blueberries, mushrooms, and tomatoes or tomato skin.

The BLW Kitchen

The BLW kitchen appears to be no unique than your normal kitchen. You don't have to have extraordinary cooking instruments to make BLW a reality. One of the benefits of utilizing BLW strategies

is that you probably as of now have the majority of what you'll
have to begin. BLW is easy,

however I prescribe a couple of staples to consistently have
available to make your experience go as flawlessly as possible.

Pantry Go-Tos

Here are a portion of my undisputed top choice storeroom
staples with regards to planning nourishment for child and the
family. However this rundown isn't comprehensive, you will see
large numbers of these fixings all through the plans in this book.
It is really smart to have these things in your storage space so
you can make fast and simple dinners or snacks in a pinch.

→ Herbs and flavors: Basil, dark pepper, ground coriander,
  ground cumin, curry powder, new garlic, garlic powder,
  Italian flavoring, onion powder, oregano, paprika,
  rosemary, sage, and salt (after child turns 1 year old)

→ Beans and vegetables: Black beans, dark looked at peas,
  chickpeas, and lentils

→ **Grains:** Egg noodles, panko bread crumbs, pasta (any type and
  shape), quinoa, rice (white or brown), rolled oats, and whole-
  wheat bread

→ Meats and protein: Low-sodium canned chicken, salmon,
  and tuna

→ **Fruits and vegetables:** Canned fruits (packed in their own
  juice), canned olives, canned tomatoes, dried fruits, and potatoes

→ Nuts and their margarines: Almonds, almond spread,
  peanuts, peanut butter, pistachios, and walnuts

→ **Oils:** Avocado oil, canola or safflower oil, olive oil, and walnut oil

Fresh and Frozen Staples

Make sure you additionally have new and frozen produce loaded

in the
cooler and cooler. I like all of the time to be ready and ready to
make something rapidly without placing an excess of thought
into it. These can be presented as a solitary food thing or can
without much of a stretch be blended in with different food
varieties. Try not to feel constrained to stock everything on the
rundown. It's simply an aide, and you can get whatever things
turn out best for your family and preferences.

→ Fresh and frozen organic product: Apples, bananas,
  blueberries, frozen blended berries, grapes, oranges,
  and strawberries

→ **Fresh and frozen vegetables:** Asparagus, avocado,
  broccoli, carrots, cauliflower, frozen edamame, frozen mixed
  vegetables, frozen peas, ginger, kale, mushrooms, onion,
  spinach, and tomatoes

→ Dairy and milk substitutes: Almond milk, cashew milk,
  cheddar, coconut milk, Colby Jack cheddar, dairy milk (for
  cooking just), full-fat Greek yogurt, kefir, oat milk,
  Parmesan cheddar, and soy milk

→ Animal and plant-based proteins: Beef or ground
  hamburger, chicken bosom or ground chicken, eggs, fish,
  ground turkey, pork hacks or ground pork, shrimp, and
  tofu

Handy Tools (Besides Baby's Hand)

Luckily, baby food is the easiest possible food to make, and BLW
makes it even snappier, especially when baby is mainly using their
hands instead of fussy spoons. However, there are some kitchen
tools that are useful during the preparation, cooking, and serving of
food.

→ Food thermometer: This significant instrument is utilized

for actually looking at the interior temperature of meat to guarantee it is appropriately cooked.

→ Vegetable peeler: This is really great for stripping the skin off of potatoes and squash, as it tends to be difficult for babies to chew.

→ Steamer container: This is utilized for steaming food varieties. Bamboo, metal, and silicone liners are for the most part similarly great and simple to use.

→ Sheet skillet: These can be utilized for baking or broiling meat or vegetables.

→ Muffin tin (smaller than normal or standard): Nonstick biscuit tins are amazingly valuable for making dinners and tidbit nibbles in a decent piece size for a little tummy.

→ **Food storage:** You'll need zip-top or silicone bags or a small set of airtight storage containers (plastic or glass) to help store leftovers or pack food when you're on the go.

→ Nonbreakable pull base dishes and placemats: Suction gets these things on the table when your child is as yet figuring out how to eat. Spills can in any case occur, however these can assist with limiting mishaps and clean-up.

→ **Self-feeding spoon:** Use this for serving food that's difficult to form into a solid shape after cooking.

→ Bibs: These will assist child with trying not to smudge their garments while eating.

→ Sippy, straw, or open cup with spilling watch: This is a preparation cup to help children to drink freely from a cup without spills.

In general, babies are developmentally ready for a sippy cup at 6 months of age and can then continue with a straw cup at about 9 months. Start off with a sippy cup that has a soft, pliable spout. You can then move up to straw cups as they require more oral motor coordination. Most babies can independently sip from an open cup when there's an adult holding it.

Once they have started eating solids, you can offer about 4 to 6 ounces of water per day. Even though you are trying to keep spills to a minimum, sometimes it's also a good opportunity for baby to experience the oopsie moment, as a reminder to drink slowly and work on improving their hand-eye coordination.

About the Recipes

This book will help you embark on your BLW adventure, guiding you as you introduce your baby to different types of foods and flavors. All of the recipes in this book are easy to make, with straightforward preparation methods and short cooking times— nearly every recipe can be made in under 35 minutes—and use everyday ingredients that you can find in grocery stores.

If you are totally new to BLW and are not sure where to start, then I recommend trying a few "starter recipes," such as Roasted Sweet Potato Sticks; Buckwheat Banana Pancakes; Berry, Applesauce, and Oatmeal Squares; Kale, Tomato, and Basil Frittata; Avocado Strips; and Steamed Kohlrabi. These plans are on the whole great decisions to launch this excursion, regardless of whether you are new to cooking.

Remember there's also the Quick-Start Guide at the beginning of the book to help guide you step by step if you feel overwhelmed.

The plans will likewise incorporate guidelines for how to serve every formula to your child, including how long to permit the food to cool and how to cut specific food varieties into proper sizes to abstain from gagging. I might likewise want to feature a couple of key elements that you'll see in the recipes:

→ **Dietary labels:** Every recipe will be marked with appropriate dietary labels, such as dairy-free, gluten-free, nut-free, soy-free, vegetarian, and vegan. You'll see something like one mark with every one of the plans to assist you with exploring which plans are the most appropriate to your child or which you might want to attempt first.

→ **Allergen names:** There's extra naming that will make you aware of normal expected allergens, like eggs, fish, shellfish, gluten, dairy, soy, and nuts.

→ **Tips:** Some plans will incorporate tips, either in the headnote or toward the finish of the formula. A few hints submit ideas for subbing a fixing or how to eliminate possible allergens. Others will give supportive cooking tips or disclose how to reuse extras in other recipes.

I genuinely want to believe that you will appreciate making the plans similarly however much I delighted in making them. Every one of the plans is nutritious while presenting child to an assortment of food sources and cultivating a positive climate for them to figure out how to eat.

Herb-Roasted Delicata Squash

CH2

6 Montths

The recipes in this section are perfect for beginner babies because they are super simple to prepare and pass the "squish test," meaning they can be easily squished between the thumb and forefinger, making them safe options for little gums. At this stage, baby will be using a palmar grasp to self-feed, so foods introduced should be cut into strips to allow for easy grabbing and holding.

<u>Avocado Strips</u> <u>Shredded Coconut–Coated Mango Wedges</u> <u>Baked Cinnamon Apple Wedges</u> <u>Steamed Green Beans with Oregano</u> <u>Steamed Kohlrabi</u> <u>Steamed Broccoli with Orange Zest</u> <u>Sautéed Zucchini with Thyme</u> <u>Roasted Sweet Potato Sticks</u> <u>Herb-Roasted Delicata Squash</u> <u>Egg and Avocado Crepe</u> <u>Easy Blueberry-Oat Blender Muffins</u> <u>Buckwheat Banana Pancakes</u>

DAIRY-FREE, GLUTEN-FREE, NUT-FREE, SOY-FREE, VEGAN
MAKES 8 STRIPS | PREP TIME: 5 MINUTES

Softandcreamyavocado isalowriskforchoking andagoodsource ofhealthyfatandcaloriesforbabiesjuststarting outwithsolid food varieties. Youcanserveavocado instrips, incubes, ormashedand placedinasiliconenonslipspoonto support self-feeding.

Avocado canbeveryslipperyandhardto getagripon, so youcan leavealittlebitofavocado skinonatthebottomforbettertraction whilebabyisholding onto it (youcanalso usethistechniquefor bananas, kiwis, pears, nectarines, andpeaches), butmakesureto keepacloseeyewhentheyareeating so theydon'teattheskin.

1 little ready avocado

1. Cut the avocado fifty-fifty and eliminate the pit. Cut every half into 4 strips or wedges with skin on.

2. Leaving around 1 inch of avocado skin at the lower part of each strip, strip off the skin from the smaller part at the top and, utilizing kitchen scissors, clip it off.

3. Serve child each avocado strip in turn. When child is beginning to snack nearer to the furthest limit of the avocado, eliminate the rest of the strip to forestall potential choking.

TIP: Avocados oxidize rapidly, so assuming that you have extras, it's ideal to track down one more use for them around the same time. (Make yourself a decent piece of avocado toast!) Alternatively, you can press some lemon juice over what remains and store it in an impenetrable holder in the cooler for up to 1 day.

DAIRY-FREE, GLUTEN-FREE, SOY-FREE, VEGAN

Allergens: NUTS

MAKES 8 WEDGES | PREP TIME: 15 MINUTES

Mango isagreatfirstfruitforbabybecauseit'ssoftandintroduces bothsweetandsourflavors. Rolling thepiecesinfinelyshredded coconutisanotherwayto helpbabygetabettergriponslippery organic products.Oncebabygetsolderandisableto pickupindividual pieces, youcancutthemango into 3D shapes. On the off chance that thecoconutflakeslooktoo coarse, puttheminafoodprocessorandpulsetheminto apowder.

1 medium mango
½ cup destroyed unsweetened coconut

1. Cut the mango on one side only away from the pit and rehash on the other three sides. You'll get 4 areas (2 greater side cuts, 2 more modest ones) and the pit, which you can discard.
2. First cut the mango into ½-inch-wide, 4-inch-long wedges with the skin on, then, at that point, run the blade under the mango tissue to eliminate the skin from each slice.
3. Put the destroyed coconut onto a plate, then, at that point, tenderly press the mango wedges into the coconut until they're well coated.
4. Serve child each mango wedge in turn. Store extras in an impermeable holder in the cooler for as long as 3 days or for as long as multi month in the freezer.

DAIRY-FREE, GLUTEN-FREE, SOY-FREE, VEGAN

Allergens: NUTS

MAKES 20 WEDGES | PREP TIME: 5 MINUTES | COOK TIME: 30 MINUTES

Cookedapplesareaversatilefirstfoodforbaby. Youcansteam, sauté, orbakethemorcookthemdownto makeapplesauce. Their skinisagoodsourceoffiber.Itwill besoftafterbaking,andyoucan leaveitonorpeel it offasdesired. Babywill spitouttheskinifthey

*don'tlikethetexture. Ifyouwantto tryserving theapplesraw,
gratethemfinelyto preventchoking.*

2 medium apples, cored and cut into ½-inch-thick wedges (about 3 cups)
1 teaspoon ground cinnamon (or to   taste)
½ teaspoon ground nutmeg
1 teaspoon coconut oil

1. Preheat the stove to 400°F.
2. Put the cut apples on a baking sheet. Add the cinnamon, nutmeg, and coconut oil and throw until the apples are uniformly covered. Orchestrate the apples on the skillet in an even layer.
3. Bake for 25 minutes, or until the apple cuts are delicate and you can without much of a stretch squash them with a fork.
4. Allow the apples to cool for 5 minutes, then, at that point, serve child each wedge in turn. Store extras in an impermeable holder in the cooler for as long as 3 days or for as long as multi month in the freezer.

TIP: You can dunk extra apple cuts in yogurt for child to attempt the following day, or cook the cuts further on the burner to make applesauce.

<u>Oregano</u>

DAIRY-FREE, GLUTEN-FREE, NUT-FREE, SOY-FREE, VEGAN
MAKES 4 (¼-CUP) PORTIONS | PREP TIME: 5 MINUTES | COOK TIME: 15 MINUTES

*Greenbeansareeasyandconvenientforbabybecausethey
alreadycomeintheperfectshape. All youhaveto do is cutthem
into 4-inch-long sticksbeforecooking. Don'tworryaboutthelittle
seedsinsidesincethey'resmall andwon'tbeachoking hazardif
swallowed.*

1 cup green beans (about 20 green   beans)
¼ teaspoon dried oregano

1. Fill a medium pan with about an inch of water and spot a liner bushel inside. Cover and heat the water to the point of boiling over medium-high heat.
2. Meanwhile, trim off the two closures of the green beans and cut them into 4-inch-long sticks.
3. Carefully place the green beans into the liner bin. Cover and cook for 12 minutes, or until the green beans become marginally olive green in shading. (You want them to be a little soft, as in fork-mashable, in the beginning when baby is starting out with solids, then you can adjust to a shorter cook time for a firmer and crunchier texture once they have more experience.) Transfer the green beans to a plate or bowl and sprinkle the oregano over them.

4. Allow the beans to cool for 2 minutes, then, at that point, serve child the beans each in turn. Store extras in a sealed shut compartment in the fridge for as long as 3 days or for as long as multi month in the freezer.

DAIRY-FREE, GLUTEN-FREE, NUT-FREE, SOY-FREE, VEGAN
MAKES 8 (¼-CUP) PORTIONS | PREP TIME: 10 MINUTES | COOK TIME: 15 MINUTES

Kohlrabiisadeliciousrootvegetablethat'softenoverlookedinthe grocerystore. Youcaneatitraworcooked. Ithasacrunchytexture andarefreshing taste in its rawstate, almostlikejicama, butwhen it's cooked, it's sweet, delicate, andjuicy. Youcaneasilyreplicatethis recipeusing otherrootvegetables, suchascarrots, beets, and daikonradish.

1 medium kohlrabi (about the size of a large onion)

1. Fill a medium pan with about an inch of water and spot a liner bushel inside. Cover and heat the water to the point of boiling over medium-high heat.
2. Cut off the leaves from the kohlrabi, then peel off the skin with a vegetable peeler or knife. Slice the kohlrabi down the middle and spot every half chopped side down on a cutting board. Cut each half into ½-inch-thick slices, then cut each slice into ½-inch-wide sticks, as you would cut a potato into French fries.
3. Carefully place the kohlrabi sticks into the liner bin. Cover and cook for 12 minutes, or until the kohlrabi is delicate and you can undoubtedly crush it with a fork.
4. Allow the kohlrabi to cool for 2 minutes, then, at that point, serve child each stick in turn. Store extras in an impenetrable compartment in the cooler for as long as 3 days or for as long as multi month in the freezer.

Zest

DAIRY-FREE, GLUTEN-FREE, NUT-FREE, SOY-FREE, VEGAN
MAKES 8 (¼-CUP) PORTIONS | PREP TIME: 5 MINUTES | COOK TIME: 10 MINUTES

Broccoliishighinfiberandagoodsourceofvitamin C, and steaming preservesthenutrientsmuchbetterthanboiling. I like to addcitruszestforadashofstrongerflavorthatstimulatesbaby's tastebuds. Youcanomittheorange zing, ifyouwish, orreplaceit withlemonzest. Beginnerbabiescanholdonto thestemofthe broccoliwhileexploring thetextureandflavoroftheflorets. Cauliflowercanbeusedinthisrecipe, aswell.

2 small heads broccoli
1 tablespoon ground orange zest

1. Fill a huge pan with about an inch of water and spot a liner crate inside. Cover and heat the water to the point of boiling over medium-high heat.
2. Trim the broccoli stalks, leaving around 2 creeps of stem for child to clutch. Cut the broccoli into ½-inch-wide florets. Cautiously place the broccoli into the liner basket.
3. Cover and cook for 7 minutes, or until the broccoli is adequately delicate to be crushed with a fork. Move the broccoli into a bowl and sprinkle the orange zing over it.
4. Allow the broccoli to cool for 3 minutes, then, at that point, serve child each floret in turn. Store extras in an impenetrable holder in the cooler for as long as 3 days or for as long as multi month in the freezer.

GLUTEN-FREE, DAIRY-FREE, NUT-FREE, SOY-FREE, VEGAN
MAKES 8 (¼-CUP) PORTIONS | PREP TIME: 10 MINUTES | COOK TIME: 15 MINUTES

Zucchinisticksareaperfecthandheldvegetable. They'rehighin fiber, whichhelpswithdigestion, andagoodsourceofmanganese forhearthealth. Thisrecipeslightlyovercooksthezucchiniso that it's easierforbabyto gumthrough.

1 tablespoon olive oil
1 teaspoon cleaved garlic (optional)
2 little zucchini, cut into ½-inch-by-3-inch
sticks 2 tablespoons water
½ teaspoon dried thyme or ½ tablespoon new thyme

1. In an enormous skillet, heat the oil over medium heat.
2. Add the garlic and sauté for 30 seconds, or until it is fragrant and brilliant brown. Add the zucchini sticks and sauté them for 2 minutes, then pour the water into the skillet. Cover and keep cooking for an additional 13 minutes, or until the zucchini is delicate and marginally soft. Sprinkle the thyme over the zucchini and throw until the thyme is well distributed.
3. Allow the zucchini to cool for 2 minutes, then, at that point, serve child each piece of zucchini in turn. Store extras in a hermetically sealed compartment in the cooler for up to 3 days.

TIP: If you are getting ready just a little part for your child, sauté just a modest bunch of zucchini sticks and store the uncooked zucchini in a water/air proof holder in the cooler for up to 1 month.

DAIRY-FREE, GLUTEN-FREE, NUT-FREE, SOY-FREE, VEGAN
MAKES 4 (¼-CUP) PORTIONS | PREP TIME: 5 MINUTES | COOK TIME: 25 MINUTES

SwEetpotatoesareaveryversatilebeginnerfoodforbaby, asthey canbesteamed, simmered, sautéed, orpureed. Theyarealso richin supplements, suchasvitamins A, E, and B6 aswell ascalciumand fiber. Fiberisimportantwhenbabystartseating solidsbecauseit canhelpwithdigestion. Feel freeto experimentwithdifferent typesofpotatoesandyamsforthisrecipe.

1 large sweet potato (about 8 ounces)
1 tablespoon olive oil
1 teaspoon paprika

1. Preheat the stove to 400°F.
2. Peel the yam. Slice the potato down the middle and spot every half chopped side down on a cutting board. Cut every half into ½-inch-thick cuts, then, at that point, cut each cut into ½-inch-wide sticks, as you would cut a potato into French fries.
3. Place the potato sticks onto a baking sheet. Add the oil and paprika and throw until the potato sticks are uniformly covered. Heat for 25 minutes, or until the potato can be handily pounded with a fork.
4. Allow the yam to cool for 2 minutes, then, at that point, serve child each stick in turn. Store extras in a water/air proof compartment in the fridge for as long as 3 days or for as long as multi month in the freezer.

TIP: You can utilize extras the following day to make crushed yams; simply add some milk or plant-based milk to make a smooth paste.

DAIRY-FREE, GLUTEN-FREE, NUT-FREE, SOY-FREE, VEGAN
MAKES 6 (¼-CUP) PORTIONS | PREP TIME: 5 MINUTES | COOK TIME: 25 MINUTES

Delicatasquashisaroundoroval-shapedsquashwitha distinctiveyellowandgreen-stripedexterior. It is little andeasyto handle. Squashisagoodsourceofenergyandfiberforalittle stomach. Theskinisedible, so youdon'thaveto spendextratime stripping it offasyouwouldwithbutternutsquash. Onceit'scooked, ithasacreamytexture, andontopofthat, it's apowerhouseof vitaminsandmineralsthatbenefitgutandhearthealth.

1 small delicata
squash 1 tablespoon

olive oil
¼ teaspoon dried sage
¼ teaspoon dried basil

1. Preheat the broiler to 375°F.
2. Cut the squash fifty-fifty. Eliminate the seeds and scratch out any wiry parts from the middle. Place the squash cut-side down on the cutting board, then cut each half into 1-inch-thick half moons. Put the cuts on a sheet container. Add the oil, sage, and basil and throw until the squash cuts are uniformly covered. Organize the squash on the container in an even layer. Heat for 20 minutes, or until the squash is delicate and you can undoubtedly pound it with a fork.
3. Allow the squash to cool for 5 minutes, then, at that point, serve child each cut in turn. Store extras in a sealed shut compartment in the fridge for as long as 3 days or for as long as multi month in the freezer.

TIP: Leftover squash can be crushed up, warmed in the microwave the following day, and filled in as a puree on a preloaded spoon.

GLUTEN-FREE, NUT-FREE, SOY-FREE, VEGETARIAN

Allergens: DAIRY, EGGS

MAKES 3 CREPES | PREP TIME: 5 MINUTES | COOK TIME: 5 MINUTES

Egg isahigh-qualityproteinandoffersavarietyofnutrients, such asiron, vitamin A, vitamin D, nutrients B6 and B12, andcholine(a keycompoundforbraindevelopmentininfantsandchildren). This egg creperecipecreatesaneasy-to-holdshapeforself-feeding.

1 large egg
2 tablespoons entire milk or plant-based milk
1 tablespoon olive oil
1 tablespoon ground cheddar or ½ tablespoon healthful yeast
½ ready avocado, mashed

1. In a medium bowl, whisk together the egg and milk until well combined.
2. In an enormous nonstick skillet, heat the oil over medium heat.
3. Place 2 to 3 tablespoons of the whisked egg into the container. Whirl the container to make a slim, 3-inch roundabout shape. Allow the crepe to cook for 20 to 30 seconds, or until set, then use a spatula to flip it over. Cook for an extra 20 to 30 seconds, or until it's totally cooked through. Move the cooked crepe to a plate and permit it to cool while you rehash this stage two additional occasions, or until all the egg combination is utilized up.
4. Starting with the principal crepe you made, sprinkle ground cheddar over each crepe and spread 1 tablespoon of pounded avocado on top.

5. Fold each crepe into a cone shape, then serve one to baby. (You can also just fold the crepe in half and cut it into 1-inch strips, then serve baby one strip at a time.) Store extras in an impermeable compartment in the fridge for up to 3 days.

Muffins

NUT-FREE, SOY-FREE, VEGETARIAN

Allergens: DAIRY, EGGS, GLUTEN

MAKES 12 MUFFINS | PREP TIME: 5 MINUTES | COOK TIME: 30 MINUTES

Muffins are a great way to introduce fruits that are smaller in size, such as blueberries. Once cooked, blueberries no longer pose a risk for choking. Blueberries are considered a superfood because they're packed with antioxidants to boost the immune system. You can certainly serve raw blueberries to child, but remember to cut them in half and smash them with a fork.

1 cup rolled oats
¾ cup entire milk or plant-based milk
1 huge egg
1 teaspoon baking powder
1 teaspoon baking soda
1 cup new or frozen blueberries

1. Preheat the broiler to 375°F.
2. Put the oats, milk, and egg into a blender and mix until smooth. Add the baking powder and baking pop and mix once more, then, at that point, overlap in the blueberries.
3. In a 12-cup nonstick biscuit tin, fill each cup 66% brimming with player. (Try not to fill the whole way to the top, to permit space for the biscuits to rise.) Bake for 25 minutes, or until a toothpick embedded into the focal point of a biscuit comes out clean.
4. Turn out the biscuits onto a wire rack and permit them to cool for 5 minutes. Cut a biscuit into 3 equivalent parts and serve child each piece in turn. If you notice your baby tends to gum off a big chunk and gag, then offer them a smaller piece instead. Store extras in an impermeable holder in the fridge for as long as 5 days or for as long as 90 days in the freezer.

TIP: You can without much of a stretch supplant the blueberries in this formula with various natural products, like strawberries, raspberries, fruit purée, or banana.

GLUTEN-FREE, NUT-FREE, SOY-FREE, VEGETARIAN

Allergens: DAIRY, EGGS

MAKES 6 PANCAKES | PREP TIME: 10 MINUTES | COOK TIME: 10 MINUTES

Buckwheatpancakesareeasyto make, easyforbabyto holdand eat, andsuitableforbabieswithaglutenallergy. Themilkandegg canbeeasilyreplacedwithplant-basedmilkandaveganegg substituteto bemorehypoallergenic.

1 cup buckwheat flour
1 teaspoon baking powder
1 teaspoon baking soda
⅔ cup entire milk or plant-based milk
1 enormous egg
2 tablespoons softened unsalted margarine, somewhat cooled 1 teaspoon vanilla extract
½ cup cut banana

1. In a huge bowl, combine as one the flour, baking powder, and baking soda.

2. In a medium bowl, combine as one the milk, egg, dissolved spread, and vanilla extract.

3. Slowly empty the wet fixings into the dry fixings and race until all around joined. The player ought to have a thick consistency, yet you should in any case have the option to pour the hitter effectively from a spoon.

4. Heat a frying pan or a nonstick skillet over medium hotness. Spoon 3 tablespoons of hitter onto the skillet. Cook for around 2 minutes, or until you see bubbles framing on the highest point of the hotcake. Place 5 cuts of banana uniformly on the hotcake, delicately squeezing them into the player. Flip the pancake over and cook for an additional 2 minutes, then transfer it to a plate. Rehash this progression with the excess player and banana.

5. Allow the flapjacks to cool for 2 minutes. Cut a pancake into ½-inch strips, then serve baby one strip at a time. Store extras in a sealed shut compartment in the cooler for as long as 5 days or for as long as multi month in the freezer.

Salmon Patties, Zesty Parmesan-Roasted Asparagus

6 tto 8 Montths

These foods should still pass the "squish test" and should be easy for baby to hold in their fist. They are still using a palmar grasp or are now using a raking grasp, so food that's in strip or stick form will still work best at this stage. Baby can also begin practicing with a spoon. You can certainly explore different spices and flavors—as long as it's not too spicy.

GLUTEN-FREE, NUT-FREE, SOY-FREE, VEGETARIAN

Allergens: DAIRY

MAKES 8 (¼-CUP) PORTIONS | PREP TIME: 10 MINUTES | COOK TIME: 15 MINUTES

Carrotsaresweetwhencooked, andthisrecipeaddslemonanddill flavorsforbabyto investigate. Ifyouthinkthiscombo is too striking, then, at that point, youcanskipthedill andlemon.

2 tablespoons unsalted butter
2 cups carrots, cut into ½-by-4-inch sticks
2 tablespoons hacked new dill, or 1 tablespoon dried dill 1
tablespoon lemon juice
1 teaspoon ground lemon zest

1. In an enormous skillet, soften the spread over medium hotness. Add the carrots and sauté for 10 minutes, or until fork-tender.

2. Stir in the dill and lemon juice. Cover and keep cooking for an additional 5 minutes, or until the carrots are delicate and you can squash them effectively with a fork. Sprinkle the lemon zing over the carrots and eliminate them from the heat.

3. Allow the carrots to cool for 2 minutes, then, at that point, serve child the cooked carrot sticks each in turn. Store extras in a water/air proof holder in the cooler for as long as 3 days or for as long as multi month in the freezer.

TIP: You can substitute or add different vegetables, like broccoli or cauliflower, and effectively adjust this formula with salted spread alongside a touch of salt and newly ground dark pepper as child gets older.

Asparagus

GLUTEN-FREE, NUT-FREE, SOY-FREE

Allergens: DAIRY

MAKES 4 (½-CUP) PORTIONS | PREP TIME: 5 MINUTES | COOK TIME: 20 MINUTES

Asparagusismygo-to vegetableforbusyfamiliesbecauseit requiresverylittlepreparationandisfull offlavorandnutrients. Aslong asyoudon'tovercookit(to thepointthatitbecomesstringy anddifficultforbabyto eat), it stayssoftandisappropriatefora half year oldinfantto munchon. To makethisdairy-freeandvegan, substitutenutritional yeastforthe Parmesan.

1 bunch asparagus, ends trimmed
1 tablespoon olive oil
2 tablespoons ground Parmesan
cheddar 1 tablespoon lemon juice
1 tablespoon ground lemon
zing Freshly ground dark
pepper

1. Preheat the broiler to 425°F.
2. In an enormous bowl, join the asparagus, oil, cheddar, and lemon squeeze and throw them together until each lance is covered. Spread the asparagus on a baking sheet in an even layer.
3. Bake for 12 to 15 minutes, or until the asparagus becomes a brilliant shade of green and is effectively sliced through with a fork. Eliminate and sprinkle lemon zing over the asparagus, and finish it off with dark pepper to taste.
4. Allow the asparagus to cool for 3 minutes. Serve child each lance in turn or cut each lance into more modest 3-inch pieces for child to get on to.

TIP: Asparagus doesn't do well more or less extras tacky when warmed. It's ideal to serve it that very day it is cooked.

GLUTEN-FREE, NUT-FREE, SOY-FREE, VEGETARIAN

Allergens: DAIRY

MAKES 2 (¼-CUP) PORTIONS | PREP TIME: 5 MINUTES | COOK TIME: 10 MINUTES

Peasareasafefoodto introduceearlyeventhoughtheyareround - mostofthemaresmall enoughnotto poseachoking hazard. For babiesupto 8 monthsold, youcanmashthem, whichmakesthem

muchsafer. Then, at that point, whenbabyisaround 9 monthsold, youcanserve themwhole.

½ cup frozen peas
½ tablespoon unsalted butter

1. Fill a little pan with about ½ inch of water and spot a liner crate inside. Cover and heat the water to the point of boiling over medium-high heat.
2. Carefully place the frozen peas into the liner crate. Cover and cook for 8 minutes, or until the peas can be effortlessly crushed with a fork.
3. Transfer the peas to a bowl, add the spread, and blend until the peas are covered. Utilizing a fork, tenderly level the peas.
4. Allow the peas to cool for 2 minutes, then serve baby the flattened peas. Child might in any case be chipping away at their pincer abilities yet should in any case have the option to get the peas with their palm and put them into their mouth. Store extras in an impenetrable holder in the cooler for as long as 3 days or for as long as multi month in the freezer.

DAIRY-FREE, GLUTEN-FREE, NUT-FREE, SOY-FREE, VEGAN
MAKES 8 (¼-CUP) PORTIONS | PREP TIME: 5 MINUTES | COOK TIME: 30 MINUTES

Cauliflowerisagoodfinger-foodvegetableforbabyto work on eating atmealtime. It's abonusthatit'salso agoodsourceof L-ascorbic acid andpotassiumandprovidessomecalciumandiron, also. Adding somecurrypowderbeforeroasting gives its flavora help. Thisdishpairswell withrice.

2 cups cauliflower florets, cut into ½-by-3-inch pieces
1 tablespoon olive oil
½ teaspoon garlic powder
½ teaspoon gentle curry powder

1. Preheat the stove to 425°F. Place the cauliflower on a baking sheet.
2. In a little bowl, whisk together the oil, garlic powder, and curry powder, then, at that point, pour it over the cauliflower and throw until the cauliflower is equally covered. Orchestrate the cauliflower on the baking sheet in an even layer.
3. Bake for 25 minutes, or until the cauliflower is delicate and you can crush the florets effectively with a fork.
4. Allow the cauliflower to cool for 5 minutes, then serve baby the florets one at a time. Some broiled cauliflower can become chewy (particularly the stem part) and will not be not difficult to slice through with a fork. Assuming that is the situation, cut it into more modest pieces prior to serving to forestall gagging. Store extras in an impermeable holder in the cooler for as long as 3 days or for as long as multi month in the freezer.

Allergens: GLUTEN

MAKES 10 STICKS | PREP TIME: 10 MINUTES | COOK TIME: 20 MINUTES

Lentilsareagreatplant-basedprotein, havegoodironcontent, and areeasyto cookcomparedwithotherdrybeans. Youdon'thaveto soakthem, whichmakesyourlifeeasierwhencooking forabusy family. Youcanalso usecannedlentils, whichmakethecooking timemuchshorterandarejustasnutritious. Lentilsarealso agood sourceofironwhenyourbabyneedsitmost, around 6 months.

½ cup lentils, rinsed and drained
½ cup rolled oats
⅛ teaspoon ground cumin (optional)
⅛ teaspoon ground cardamom (optional)

1. Put the lentils in a 4-quart pot and cover them with water. Heat the water to the point of boiling over high hotness. When the water is bubbling, lessen the hotness to low and stew for around 20 minutes, or until the lentils are delicate and can be effectively crunched between your fingers. Channel the water and permit the lentils to cool for 2 minutes.

2. Put the oats in a food processor and pound them. Add the cumin (if utilizing), cardamom (if utilizing), and cooked lentils, and heartbeat until the fixings are very much consolidated. (It should appear as though a thick tomato glue. In the event that it's runny, add more oats to the mixture.)

3. Scoop out 1 piling tablespoon of the lentil combination into your hand and structure it into a ½-inch-wide finger-formed stick. Serve child the lentil bars each in turn. Store extras in a sealed shut compartment in the fridge for as long as 5 days or for as long as 90 days in the freezer.

TIP: I use cumin and cardamom in the blend, however you can forget about them or supplant them with sweet flavors, for example, pumpkin-pie zest, nutmeg, or cinnamon, if desired.

Allergens: DAIRY, EGGS, GLUTEN

MAKES 12 MUFFINS | PREP TIME: 5 MINUTES | COOK TIME: 25 MINUTES

Flaxseedishighinfiberandmagnesiumandisagreatadditionto thismuffinto helpmovebaby'sbowels. Flaxseedalso contains omega-3s, whicharegoodfortheheartandbrain. Thisrecipecan beeasilyadaptedusing nondairymilkandyogurtorveganeggs to avoidthoseallergens, ifneeded. Oncebabyisoveroneyearold, you

canadd 1 or 2 tablespoonsofmaplesyrupinstep 2 to sweetenita little bit.

1⅔ cups rolled oats
1 cup whole milk
½ cup full-fat vanilla Greek yogurt
⅓ cup ground flaxseed or flaxseed feast
1 teaspoon baking powder
1 teaspoon baking soft
drink 1 enormous egg
1 cup new or frozen raspberries

1. Preheat the stove to 400°F.
2. In a food processor or blender, join the oats, milk, yogurt, flaxseed, baking powder, baking pop, and egg. Mix on high until a fluid player structures. Utilizing an elastic spatula, delicately crease the raspberries into the batter.
3. In a 12-cup nonstick biscuit tin, fill each cup 66% loaded with player. (Try not to fill the whole way to the top, to permit space for the biscuits to rise.) Bake for 20 minutes, or until a toothpick embedded into the focal point of a biscuit comes out clean.
4. Turn out the biscuits onto a wire rack and permit them to cool for 5 minutes. Cut a biscuit into 3 equivalent parts and serve child each piece in turn. Store extras in a sealed shut holder in the cooler for as long as 5 days or for as long as 90 days in the cooler. Freeze them separately first and afterward put them in a water/air proof compartment to keep them from staying together.

Peanut Butter

DAIRY-FREE, VEGAN

Allergens: GLUTEN, NUTS, SOY

MAKES 2 WAFFLES | PREP TIME: 5 MINUTES | COOK TIME: 15 MINUTES

It's notrecommendedto givebabiespeanutbutterstraightoutof thejarbecauseit'sthickandsticky, whichcancausegagging and hurling. So tryadding meltedpeanutbutterorpeanutpowder to foodssuchaswaffles, biscuits, andpancakes. Youcaneasily switchoutdifferenttypesofnutbutterornutpowder, aswell. If youdon'thaveawaffleironathome, simplyadd 2 teaspoons baking powderto themixtureandusethebatterforpancakes.

2 tablespoons creamy salted peanut butter 2 cups rolledoats
2 ready bananas, squashed (⅔ cup to 1 cup)
1½ cups soy milk or other plant-based milk

1. Heat a waffle iron on high heat.

2. Put the peanut butter on a microwave-safe saucer, and microwave it for 30 seconds. Stir it, then microwave it for another 30 seconds, or until it reaches a melted-honey- like consistency or until it is no longer thick and sticky.

3. In a blender or food processor, join the oats, bananas, soy milk, and peanut butter. Mix on high until a hitter forms.

4. Pour the player into the waffle iron. Cook until the external edges are brilliant brown and firm, around 5 minutes. Rehash this progression until all of the player has been used.

5. Let the waffles cool for 3 minutes, then, at that point, cut them into ½-inch-wide strips and serve child each strip in turn. Store extras in an impenetrable holder in the cooler for as long as 5 days or for as long as 90 days in the freezer.

MAKES 4 (¼-CUP) PORTIONS | PREP TIME: 5 MINUTES, PLUS OVERNIGHT TO CHILL

This super simple recipe is best to prep the night before so you'll have breakfast ready to go in the morning. Chia seeds soften up when soaked in liquid, but don't serve unsoaked chia to baby as it's a choking danger. You can use a variety of toppings on this dish, including grated vegetables or chopped fruits. Since the mixture will be thicker, you can let baby try eating it either with a spoon or with their hands for some sensory exposure.

⅓ cup rolled oats
⅓ cup entire milk or plant-based milk
1 teaspoon chia seeds
2 tablespoons full-fat lemon Greek yogurt
2 tablespoons hacked strawberries or slashed product of decision (slice to ½ inch or smaller)

1. In a 8-ounce glass container, consolidate the oats, milk, chia seeds, and yogurt and mix until all around joined. Cover the top with the cleaved strawberries.

2. Refrigerate the oat blend for the time being. Assuming you track down that the oat and chia combination has become too thick in the first part of the day, you can thin it out with extra milk prior to serving it to baby.

3. Serve the oats in a bowl and let child use their hands, or preload a spoon and let them serve themselves. Store extras in a sealed shut holder in the cooler for up to 3 days.

MAKES 4 (½-CUP) PORTIONS | PREP TIME: 5 MINUTES | COOK TIME: 25 MINUTES

Manypeoplewonderhowyoucanintroducecornto ababysince cornkernelscanbeachoking hazardatsuchayoung age. Polenta, orcornmeal mush, isagreatoption. Thisisaquickversionof polenta, anditmaystill beslightlygrittyintexture. Ifyouwant moreofacreamytexture, whiskitfor 10 minuteslonger.

2 cups whole milk
½ cup cornmeal
½ tablespoon unsalted spread
1 cup ground Parmesan
cheese

1. In a little pot, heat the milk to the point of boiling over medium hotness. When the milk is bubbling, continuously race in the cornmeal. Diminish the hotness to medium-low and keep cooking for around 20 minutes, blending much of the time, until the combination thickens and the cornmeal is a soft surface. Assuming that the cornmeal begins to bubble excessively, turn the hotness to low.

2. Once the combination has thickened, add the margarine and Parmesan, and keep blending until the spread has melted.

3. Scoop out a ½-cup segment and permit it to cool for 5 minutes prior to stacking some onto a little child spoon. Hand the spoon to child and permit them to take care of themself. Store extra polenta in a hermetically sealed holder in the cooler for up to 5 days.

TIP: Polenta will solidify much more subsequent to being in the fridge short-term. You can then cut it into strips or wedges and sear it with a little olive oil. It's best not to freeze polenta as it will in general delivery a ton of water.

Patties

MAKES 8 PATTIES | PREP TIME: 10 MINUTES | COOK TIME: 20 MINUTES

Turkeyisaleanproteinandasourceofironforbaby. It's likewise an excellentsourceof Bvitaminsandthemineral selenium, whichis importantforbrainhealth. Youcanservebabycookedturkey breastthat'ssoakedinbroth, ortrythiseasyturkeyandapple wiener pattythattheentirefamilycanenjoy(feel freeto salt pattiesforotherfamilymemberswhilecooking).

8 ounces lean ground turkey
⅔ cup finely hacked apples, with or without skin
1 teaspoon dried sage
⅛ teaspoon newly ground dark pepper 2
tablespoons canola oil

1. In a medium bowl, combine as one the ground turkey, apples, sage, and pepper.

2. Scoop 2 tablespoons of the turkey blend into your hand and structure it into a ball, then, at that point, straighten it somewhat with your palm to frame a ½-inch-thick patty. Rehash this progression until all of the turkey combination has been used.

3. In a huge skillet, heat the oil over medium hotness. At the point when it begins to shimmer, place a couple of patties in the skillet (don't stuff the container) and fry the patties for 5 minutes on each side, or until the inward temperature arrives at 165°F.

4. Cut one patty into ½-inch strips and allow it to cool for 5 minutes, then serve baby one strip at a time. Store extra patties in a hermetically sealed holder in the cooler for as long as 3 days or for as long as multi month in the freezer.

TIP: You can undoubtedly slash up extra patties and make frankfurter fried eggs for breakfast the following day. Or on the other hand make a little turkey burger for more seasoned children.

DAIRY-FREE, NUT-FREE, SOY-FREE

Allergens: EGGS, FISH, GLUTEN

MAKES 8 PATTIES | PREP TIME: 10 MINUTES | COOK TIME: 10 MINUTES

Salmonisknownasabrainfooddueto its omega-3 substance. Insteadofmaking patties, youcancertainlyjustgivebabysmall piecesofflakedsalmon, yet I like to makeitinto pattiesto further support theirhand, eye, andmouthcoordination. Youcanuse freshcookedsalmonifyouareinacoastal areawherefreshsalmon canbeeasilyobtained. Somemayonnaisecontainssoyoil, so check theingredientsifbabyhasanallergy.

1 (14.5-ounce) can reduced-sodium salmon, without bones, rinsed and drained
½ cup panko bread crumbs
¼ cup mayonnaise
1 tablespoon lemon juice
1 enormous egg
½ teaspoon garlic powder
⅛ teaspoon ginger powder or 1 teaspoon ground new ginger
(discretionary) 1 teaspoon paprika

2 tablespoons canola oil

1. Squeeze out any abundance fluid from the salmon and spot it in a huge blending bowl.
2. Add the bread scraps, mayonnaise, lemon juice, egg, garlic powder, ginger (if utilizing), and paprika and mix until very much consolidated. Scoop 2 tablespoons of the combination into your hand and structure it into a patty. Rehash until all of the blend has been used.
3. In a huge skillet, heat the oil over medium hotness. Place the patties in the dish and fry them for 5 minutes on each side, or until warmed through and brilliant brown.
4. Allow the patties to cool for 5 minutes, then serve baby a whole patty, or cut one patty into ½-inch strips and serve baby one strip at a time. Store leftovers in an airtight container in the refrigerator for up to 3 days, or freeze them on a sheet pan, then place them in an airtight container to prevent them from sticking together, and store in the freezer for up to 1 month.

TIP: Salmon patties can without much of a stretch be changed into burgers for grown-ups or older
kids. Or you can mix leftovers into Mixed Vegetable Rice Balls.

DAIRY-FREE, GLUTEN-FREE, NUT-FREE, SOY-FREE
MAKES 8 STRIPS | PREP TIME: 5 MINUTES | COOK TIME: 30 MINUTES

Chicken can be served to baby as long as it's moist and can be mashed easily with a fork. Poaching chicken in liquid will forestall the meat from becoming dry and tough. If you think baby can handle a bit more flavor, sprinkle some oregano, garlic, paprika, or onion powder on the chicken.

4 cups water
4 ounces boneless, skinless chicken breast
1 flimsy cut new ginger or ½ teaspoon ginger powder
2 garlic cloves
1 scallion, green part only

1. Fill a little pot with the water and heat it to the point of boiling over medium-high heat.
2. Once the water has bubbled, add the chicken, ginger, garlic, and scallion. Cover and let the water reach boiling point once more. Then, at that point, lessen the hotness to low and stew for 20 minutes.
3. Check the chicken with a thermometer to ensure it arrives at an interior temperature of 165°F.
4. Remove the chicken from the water (save the stock for another utilization) and permit it to cool for 5 minutes prior to cutting it into ½-inch strips. Serve child one strip at a time.
5. Store extras in a sealed shut compartment in the cooler for up to 3 days.

DAIRY-FREE, GLUTEN-FREE, NUT-FREE, SOY-FREE, VEGAN
MAKES 12 MUFFINS | PREP TIME: 5 MINUTES | COOK TIME: 30 MINUTES

Quinoaispackedwithplant-basedproteinandfiber; italso containsgoodsourcesofiron, selenium, zinc, andcopper, all of whichareimportantforredbloodcell productionandimmune systemregulation. Sincequinoaissmall, soft, anddrywhenit's cooked, it's bestto serveinamuffinbiteforlittlehandsto hold. You don'thaveto useveganeggs ifyoudon'tneedto; justsubstitute with 3 enormous eggs instead.

1 (14.5-ounce) container low-sodium vegetable broth
1 cup quinoa
1 cup veggie lover fluid eggs
½ teaspoon garlic powder
½ teaspoon onion powder
½ teaspoon paprika
1 cup finely slashed broccoli

1. Preheat the stove to 375°F.

2. In a little pot, join the stock and the quinoa and heat to the point of boiling over medium-high hotness. Cover, diminish the hotness to low, and stew for 10 minutes, or until all the stock is retained. Switch off the hotness and eliminate the skillet from the stove.

3. Slowly speed in the veggie lover eggs, garlic powder, onion powder, paprika, and broccoli until all around joined. In a 12-cup nonstick biscuit tin, fill each cup with the egg combination. Heat for 15 minutes, or until the quinoa appears as though clear yellow pearls.

4. Turn the biscuits out onto a wire rack and permit them to cool for 5 minutes. Serve child an entire biscuit, or cut a biscuit into 3 pieces and serve child each piece in turn. Assuming it is still delicate and self-destructs, let it cool for 5 extra minutes so it solidifies up marginally and is simpler for child to eat. Store extras in a hermetically sealed holder in the fridge for as long as 3 days or for as long as multi month in the freezer.

DAIRY-FREE, GLUTEN-FREE, NUT-FREE, SOY-FREE, VEGETARIAN

Allergens: EGGS

MAKES 2 (¼-CUP) PORTIONS | PREP TIME: 5 MINUTES | COOK TIME: 10 MINUTES

Youcanservethisoversoftnoodles, delicate rice, or riceporridge

to makeitheartierforadultsorolderchildren. Thetartnessofthe tomatoeswiththescrambledeggs is flavorful.Ifyoulike,sprinkle someshredded Parmesancheeseoverthetopbeforeserving,butit wouldmaketherecipeno longerdairy-freeorvegetarian.

½ tablespoon olive
oil 2 large eggs,
beaten
⅓ cup slashed tomatoes, drained

1. In an enormous nonstick skillet, heat the oil over medium-high hotness. When the oil is hot, lessen the hotness to medium.

2. Pour in the eggs and cook, delicately blending, for around 2 minutes. When the eggs begin to set, add the hacked tomatoes and continue to mix for an additional 2 minutes. Switch off the hotness once the eggs are no longer runny.

3. Allow the eggs to cool for 2 minutes. Serve child a ¼-cup segment in a bowl and let child use their hands, or preload a spoon and let them work on taking care of themself.

TIP: It's ideal to eat this dish soon after it's cooked on the grounds that the tomato will keep on delivering a ton of fluid whenever left in the fridge short-term. In the event that you wouldn't fret the abundance fluid, you can store extras in a sealed shut holder in the fridge for up to 3 days.

Nutritional Yeast

DAIRY-FREE, GLUTEN-FREE, NUT-FREE, VEGAN

Allergens: SOY

MAKES 5 STICKS | PREP TIME: 5 MINUTES | COOK TIME: 15 MINUTES

Tofuisagoodsourceofplantproteinandironaswell ascalcium, whichisessential forbaby'sgrowthandbones. Thetextureissoft, yettheshapeissolidenoughforbabyto holdintheirhandforself-taking care of. Thenutritional yeastisjustto addextraflavoranda nutrient Bboost.Ifyoudon'tlikenutritional yeast,no issue just useshredded Parmesancheese(whichwouldmakethisrecipeno longerdairy-freeorvegan) orsomegarlic andonionpowder instead.

1 tablespoon canola oil
1 square medium-firm tofu, cut into 5 (⅔-by-4-inch)
pieces 1 tablespoon nourishing yeast

1. In an enormous nonstick skillet, heat the oil over medium heat.

2. Using a paper towel, wipe off each piece of tofu to limit oil splatter when it hits the container. Carefully slide the tofu into the pan and lightly fry it for about 3 minutes, then flip it over and fry for 3 minutes more, or until the whole exterior is a light golden brown but not hard or crisp.

3. Move the tofu to a plate and sprinkle the healthful yeast over the top.

4. Allow the tofu to cool for 5 minutes, then, at that point, serve child each stick of tofu in turn. Store extras in an impenetrable holder in the cooler for up to 3 days.

TIP: You can cut extra tofu into blocks and use in Tofu, Cabbage, Carrot, and Noodle Stir-Fry.

Kale, Tomato, and Basil Frittata

CH4

9 tto 12 Montths

The recipes in this section will help baby transition to and explore more complex foods while still focusing on important nutrients, like iron and calcium, and healthy fats. At this age, baby is beginning to practice their pincer skills to pick up small pieces of food. You can start cutting food into small pieces (¼- to ½-inch cubes) or continue cutting food into strips if appropriate.

Sautéed Collard Greens Broiled
Portabella with Parmesan Kale,
Tomato, and Basil Frittata
Fork-Mashed Chickpea and Avocado Salad
Berry, Applesauce, and Oatmeal Squares
Black-and-White Sesame Avocado Toast
Pizza Toast with Olives and Mushrooms
Mixed Vegetable Rice Balls   Easy Chicken
Noodle Soup Rice Pilaf with Black-Eyed
Peas Savory Beef Meatballs Ground Pork,
Basil, and Cilantro Patties Panfried Tofu
Shrimp Sticks Green Pesto Bow-Tie Pasta
Penne Pasta with Ground Walnut Alfredo Sauce

DAIRY-FREE, GLUTEN-FREE, NUT-FREE, SOY-FREE, VEGAN
MAKES 6 (¼-CUP) PORTIONS | PREP TIME: 5 MINUTES | COOK TIME: 10 MINUTES

Leafygreensarepackedwithantioxidantsandvitamins. Theyare bestservedto babycookedandchoppedbecauselong stripsor stringyvegetablescaneasilymakethemgag if theyaren't swallowedproperly. Collardgreensaremildinflavorandeasyto cook. Youcancertainlyservethisrecipesooner, butit's flimsyonce cooked, anditishardforyoung infantsto guidefoodinto theirown mouthswhentheirpincerskillsarenotyetdeveloped, whichcan causefrustration. Ifyoudo decideto servesautéedleafyveggies earlyon, chopthemsmall andserveonaspooninstead.

1 tablespoon olive oil
1 teaspoon hacked garlic
1 pack collard greens, cut into 1-inch strips, then, at that point, chopped
¼ cup apple juice vinegar

1. In an enormous skillet, heat the oil over medium hotness. Add the hacked garlic and cook for around 30 seconds, mixing, or until the garlic starts becoming brilliant brown.

2. Add the collard greens and cook, blending, until the passes on start to shrivel. Add the apple juice vinegar, cover, and cook for around 5 minutes, or until the collards become a brilliant shade of green.

3. Allow the greens to cool for 2 minutes, then scoop a ¼-cup portion into a bowl and let baby eat it with a fork, a spoon, or their fingers. Store extras in a hermetically sealed holder in the fridge for as long as 3 days or for as long as multi month in the freezer.

TIP: You can without much of a stretch warm extras in the microwave or throw them into Kale, Tomato, and Basil Frittata.

GLUTEN-FREE, NUT-FREE, SOY-FREE

Allergens: DAIRY

MAKES 5 STRIPS | PREP TIME: 5 MINUTES | COOK TIME: 10 MINUTES

Portabellamushroomsareaneasyfingerfoodto deal to child whentheyreach 9 monthsofage. Mushroomscanbechewywhen cooked, butportabellasremainfairlysoftandeasyto eat, regardless of whether babyhasteethornot. Ifyouareworriedaboutthembiting offabig lump, cutthemushroominto smallercubesandletthempractice theirpincerskills.

1 portabella mushroom cap
½ tablespoon olive oil
¼ cup ground Parmesan cheese
½ teaspoon oregano

1. Preheat the stove to 400°F.

2. Remove the stem of the mushroom, however leave the gills in. Brush the oil all around the cap and gills and spot the mushroom in a baking container gill-side up.

3. Cook for 10 minutes, or until the mushroom is delicate and turns a most unfathomable brown-dark tone. Move the mushroom to a plate and sprinkle the Parmesan cheddar and oregano over the top.

4. Allow the mushroom to cool for 2 minutes, then, at that point, cut it into ½-to 1-inch-thick

pieces and serve child each strip in turn. Store extras in a sealed shut compartment in the fridge for up to 3 days.

MAKES 8 WEDGES | PREP TIME: 10 MINUTES | COOK TIME: 20 MINUTES

Frittatasareanutritiousbreakfastfoodfortheentirefamily. They areincrediblyversatile, so feel freeto trythiswithyourfavorite fixings andvegetables. I likemaking frittatas inacast-iron skillet, butyoucanalso baketheminamuffintinat 350°F for 20 minutes(oruntil completelyset) foreasyportioncontrol.

8 large eggs
½ cup entire milk
2 tablespoons olive oil
1 cup cleaved kale
⅔ cup quartered cherry tomatoes
½ cup slashed new basil
½ cup ground Parmesan cheese

1. In a huge blending bowl, whisk together the eggs and milk.
2. In a medium cast-iron skillet, heat the oil over medium hotness. Add the kale and tomatoes and sauté for 2 minutes, or until the kale has started to shrivel. Add the basil and cook for 1 extra moment. Empty the egg combination into the dish and mix to equitably disseminate the vegetables. Cook for around 15 minutes, or until the substance have totally set. Top with the Parmesan cheese.
3. Cut the frittata into 8 wedges. Allow the frittata to cool for 3 minutes, then serve baby one wedge, cutting into smaller pieces as needed. Store extras in a water/air proof holder in the fridge for as long as 3 days or for as long as multi month in the freezer.

TIP: You can easily reheat leftover frittata in the microwave to serve as a snack the next day, or you can chop it up and mix it into Rice Pilaf with Black-Eyed Peas.

MAKES 6 (½-CUP) PORTIONS | PREP TIME: 5 MINUTES

I enjoythissimplerecipewithavocado cubesbecauseitallows babyto practicetheirpincerskillsalong withhand-eye coordination. Inthisrecipe, I usecannedchickpeas; ifyouwantto usedriedchickpeas, you'll needto soakthemovernight, cookthem for 45 minutesto anhour, andthendrainandletthemcool before using.

1 (15.5-ounce) can chickpeas, flushed and
depleted 1 medium ready avocado, pitted and
cubed
1 teaspoon olive oil
1 teaspoon lemon juice
1 teaspoon ground lemon zest
1 tablespoon hacked new parsley

1. Put the chickpeas in a huge bowl. Utilizing a fork, squash them somewhat without making them into a mush.

2. Add the cubed avocado, oil, lemon juice, lemon zing, and parsley. Throw until the fixings are well mixed.

3. Serve child a ½-cup segment, which they can eat with their hands, or they can work on utilizing a spoon. Store extras in an impenetrable compartment in the cooler for as long as 5 days or for as long as multi month in the freezer.

TIP: You can reuse this formula by placing the extras into a blender and showering in more olive oil (around 1½ tablespoons per ½ cup of the chickpea combination) to transform this into an avocado hummus spread or dip.

DAIRY-FREE, SOY-FREE, VEGAN

Allergens: GLUTEN, NUTS

MAKES 12 SQUARES | PREP TIME: 5 MINUTES | COOK TIME: 30 MINUTES

Oatsareagoodsourceofiron, magnesium, zinc, andfiber-particularlybetaglucanfiber, whichhasimmune-regulating effectsandalso promotesguthealth. Pleaserememberthatbaby shouldn'tbeeating driedfruitswhole, andinthisrecipe, the cranberriesarechoppedso they'renotachoking danger.Youcan usechoppedstrawberriesorblackberriesinsteadofblueberries, if desired.

1 cup rolled oats
½ cup fruit purée or crushed banana
¼ cup coconut milk or other plant-based milk
½ cup new or frozen blueberries
¼ cup dried unsweetened cranberries, chopped

1. Preheat the broiler to 350°F. Daintily oil a 8-by-6-inch baking pan.

2. In a huge bowl, combine as one the oats, fruit purée, and coconut milk. Overlay in the blueberries and dried cranberries until they are equally distributed.

3. Transfer the oat blend into the pre-arranged baking container and spread it out

evenly.

4. Bake for 30 minutes, or until the top is marginally brown. Permit to cool for 2 minutes. Then cut into 2-inch squares or 1-by-2-inch strips and serve baby one square or strip at a time. Store extras in a hermetically sealed compartment in the cooler for as long as 5 days or for as long as multi month in the freezer.

MAKES 2 TOASTS | PREP TIME: 5 MINUTES | COOK TIME: 5 MINUTES

Avocado toasthasbecomeago-to dinner. Thegoodnewsisthatthis isadishyouandbabycanenjoytogether! Thisrecipeisagoodway to startintroducing seedsinto baby'sdiet. Sesameseedsaresmall androundenoughto notbeachoking hazard. Youcanboostthe flavorsandvarythetextureofthisdishbyadding garnishes, suchas choppedhard-boiledeggs, garlic powder, ornutritional yeast.

1 slice whole-wheat bread
1 little ready avocado, pitted and mashed
¼ teaspoon white sesame seeds
¼ teaspoon dark sesame seeds

1. Place the bread into a toaster, on a frying pan, or in a dish and delicately toast it for 2 minutes. You want to toast only one side.
2. Once the toast is prepared, spread the crushed avocado on the toasted side and sprinkle the sesame seeds uniformly over the top.
3. Trim off the bread outsides and cut each toast into 4 equivalent parts. Serve child one piece at a time.

MAKES 2 TOASTS | PREP TIME: 10 MINUTES | COOK TIME: 10 MINUTES

Pizzatoastisaneasylunchordinnerforbabyandothertoddlers. It's arecipewithunlimitedoptions. Simplyswapouttheolivesand mushroomsforanyothervegetablesyouwantbabyto try.

2 slices whole-wheat toast
¼ cup tomato sauce

½ **cup destroyed mozzarella cheese**
¼ **cup cut dark olives**
¼ **cup cut cremini or fasten mushrooms**

1. Preheat the stove broiler.

2. Place the bread into a toaster, on a frying pan, or in a dish and gently toast it for 2 minutes. The bread ought to be simply somewhat solidified prior to becoming brown. Place the lightly toasted bread on a baking sheet, then spread the tomato sauce evenly over each piece. Sprinkle half of the mozzarella cheddar onto each piece, trailed by half of the dark olives and mushrooms.

3. Place the baking sheet under the grill and cook for 5 minutes, or until all the cheddar has melted.

4. Allow the pizzas to cool for 3 minutes to allow the cheddar to set. Trim off the coverings and cut the toasts into 1-inch strips. Serve child one strip at a time.

DAIRY-FREE, GLUTEN-FREE, NUT-FREE, SOY-FREE, VEGAN
MAKES 15 RICE BALLS | PREP TIME: 5 MINUTES | COOK TIME: 30 MINUTES

Riceballsaresimpleandversatile. Youcanaddorswapinleftover vegetablesandmeatto maketheseacomplete, nutritiousmeal for child. I personallyliketo addleftoversalmonandcrumbledroasted seaweedto themix. Ifyouarenervousabouttheroundshapeasa gagging peril, justbreakoffsmallerpiecesforthemto pickup.

1 **cup short-grain or sushi rice**
1½ **cups water**
⅔ **cup finely hacked carrots**
⅔ **cup finely cleaved broccoli**

1. Rinse and channel the rice, then, at that point, put it in a medium saucepan.

2. Add the water and heat it to the point of boiling over high hotness. When the water is bubbling, lessen the hotness to low, cover, and stew for around 5 minutes. Add the carrots and broccoli (without mixing), cover, and stew for 8 extra minutes, or until the vegetables are delicate and the rice is clear, delicate, and cushy. (Assuming the rice is still hard, add 3 tablespoons water and let it cook on low hotness for another 5 minutes.)

3. Mix the vegetables into the rice.

4. Allow the rice and vegetables to cool for around 5 minutes, then, at that point, scoop 2 tablespoons of the blend into your hand and structure a ball. Rehash with the excess rice.

5. Cut a rice ball into quarters and serve child each piece in turn. Store extras in a sealed shut holder in the fridge for as long as 3 days. Make a point to warm the rice balls in a liner or microwave, as cool rice is hard and crumbly.

Allergens: EGGS, GLUTEN

MAKES 8 (1-CUP) PORTIONS | PREP TIME: 5 MINUTES | COOK TIME: 35 MINUTES

Chickennoodlesoupisaneasymeal to makefortheentirefamily. Rememberthechickenbrothfromthe Poached Chicken*recipe? Youcanuseitupinthissoup, whichisagreatwayto reuse leftovers.*

1 tablespoon olive oil
½ cup cleaved yellow or red onion
1 cup slashed carrots
1 cup hacked celery
3 garlic cloves
2 cove leaves
4 cups chicken broth (see here) or 1 (32-ounce) container low-sodium or no-salt
  chicken stock
2 cups water
2 cups egg noodles
1 cup destroyed or cubed cooked chicken
¼ cup slashed new parsley

1. Fill an enormous stockpot 66% loaded with water and heat the water to the point of boiling over medium-high heat.

2. While the water is reaching boiling point, in a medium stockpot, heat the oil over medium hotness. Add the onion, carrots, and celery and sauté until the onion is clear, around 5 minutes. Add the garlic and narrows leaves and keep sautéing for one more moment. Pour in the chicken stock and water and carry it to a boil.

3. Once the water in the enormous pot has reached boiling point, add the egg noodles and cook them for 5 minutes (the noodles ought not be totally cooked through). Channel the noodles and set them aside.

4. Once the soup is bubbling, decrease the hotness to low, cover, and stew for 10 minutes.

5. Add the cooked egg noodles and the cooked chicken to the soup. Keep on stewing for an additional 5 minutes to let the egg noodles absorb the flavor and get done with cooking. Sprinkle in the parsley.

6. Ladle a 1-cup segment into a bowl for child and permit it to cool for 5 minutes. Urge child to work on utilizing a child fork or spork, or they can keep on utilizing their fingers, as wanted. Store extras in a hermetically sealed compartment in the cooler for as long as 3 days or for as long as multi month in the freezer.

TIP: If you are putting away the soup in the cooler, make a point to fill the holder simply 66% full to permit space for extension during freezing. On the off chance that you pack it, the glass or plastic compartment might break or part open.

Peas

DAIRY-FREE, GLUTEN-FREE, NUT-FREE, SOY-FREE, VEGAN
MAKES 6 (½-CUP) PORTIONS | PREP TIME: 5 MINUTES | COOK TIME: 30 MINUTES

Ataround 10 monthsofage, baby'shand-eyecoordinationskills improve, andtheycanbeginto holdaspoonandscooppricefromthe bowl orplateinto theirmouthmoresuccessfully. I likeblack-peered toward peasbecausetheydon'trequireaslong asoaking timeandcook relativelyquickly. Inthisrecipe, I usecannedbeansto savetime, butyoucancertainlyusedriedblack-eyedpeasandcookthemina pressurecookeroronthestovetopfor 35 to 40 minutes.

1 cup long-grain rice
2 cups low-sodium vegetable broth
1½ cups canned dark peered toward peas, washed and drained

1. Rinse and channel the rice, then, at that point, put it in a medium pot. Place the skillet on the oven, add the stock, and heat it to the point of boiling over medium-high heat.

2. Once it's bubbling, decrease the hotness to medium-low, cover, and stew for 20 minutes. Reveal and add the canned dark looked at peas, overlay them into the rice, and cover and cook for an additional 5 minutes. When all the broth is absorbed, the black-eyed peas are warm, and the rice is soft, then it's done.

3. Scoop a ½-cup segment into a bowl and permit it to cool for 3 minutes. Preload a spoon and let child serve themself, or they can utilize their hands. Store extras in a water/air proof holder in the fridge for as long as 3 days or for as long as multi month in the freezer.

NUT-FREE, SOY-FREE

Allergens: DAIRY, EGGS, GLUTEN

MAKES 8 MEATBALLS | PREP TIME: 10 MINUTES | COOK TIME: 20 MINUTES

Youcanflattenthesemeatballsinto pattiesormaketheminto linksbeforecooking themfor 9-month-oldbabiesandmoveupto meatball shapeataround a year.Youcanchooseto eitherbake orpanfrythese, whicheversuitsyourpreference.

1 pound 90% lean ground beef
¼ cup bread crumbs
½ cup destroyed Parmesan cheddar
(discretionary) 1 enormous egg
2 tablespoons entire milk or plant-based milk

½ **teaspoon garlic powder**
½ **teaspoon onion powder**
2 teaspoons Italian seasoning

1. Preheat the broiler to 400°F. Line a baking sheet with material paper.
2. In a huge bowl, combine as one the hamburger, bread pieces, Parmesan (if utilizing), egg, milk, garlic powder, onion powder, and Italian seasoning.
3. Scoop up 2 storing tablespoons of the combination and structure it into a meatball, patty, or connection. Place it on the pre-arranged baking sheet. Rehash this progression with the leftover meat combination, dispersing the meatballs essentially ½ inch separated on the baking sheet.
4. Bake for 20 minutes, or until the meatballs are cooked through and the inner temperature arrives at 165°F.
5. Cut a meatball into 3 equivalent parts and permit it to cool for 2 minutes. Serve child each piece in turn. Store extra meatballs in a hermetically sealed holder in the cooler for as long as 3 days or for as long as multi month in the freezer.

TIP: Meatballs can be warmed effectively in the microwave and matched with various plunging sauces for more flavor exposure.

Cilantro Patties

DAIRY-FREE, GLUTEN-FREE, NUT FREE, SOY-FREE

Allergens: EGGS

MAKES 10 PATTIES | PREP TIME: 10 MINUTES | COOK TIME: 10 MINUTES

Groundporkpattiesareagoodwayto introduceiron-richfoodto child. Youcanmixinchoppedvegetables, suchascarrotsand cabbage, orherbs, suchasparsley, to createdifferentflavor mixes. Onceyourbabyisover 1 yearold, youcanadda pinchofsaltto themixtureto improvetheflavororallowbabyto dunkapattyinthedipping sauceofyour-ortheir-choice.

1 pound ground pork
½ **teaspoon garlic powder**
½ **teaspoon onion powder**
½ **cup hacked new basil**
½ **cup cleaved new cilantro 1**
huge egg
2 tablespoons water
2 tablespoons canola oil

1. In an enormous bowl, combine as one the pork, garlic powder, onion powder,

basil, cilantro, egg, and water.

2. Scoop up 2 tablespoons of meat combination, structure it into a patty, and spot it on a plate. Rehash this progression until all of the meat blend is spent; you ought to have 10 patties.

3. In an enormous skillet, heat the oil over medium hotness. Organize the patties in the container with the goal that they are not contacting one another. Cook them for 5 minutes on each side, or until they are cooked through and the inward temperature arrives at 165°F.

4. Cut one patty into 3 equivalent strips and permit it to cool for 5 minutes. Serve child each strip in turn. Store extras in an impenetrable holder in the fridge for as long as 3 days or for as long as multi month in the freezer.

DAIRY-FREE, GLUTEN-FREE, NUT-FREE

Allergens: EGGS, SHELLFISH, SOY

MAKES 8 STICKS | PREP TIME: 10 MINUTES | COOK TIME: 15 MINUTES

Thisisaneasywayto introduceshellfishto yourbaby. The ingredientsareblendedinto apaste, formedinto anyshapeyou like, thenpanfried. It's nowrecommendedto introduceshellfish, suchasshrimp, earlyonto avoidfutureallergies.

1½ cups peeled and deveined shrimp
1 (3-by-3-inch) block firm tofu, depleted and cubed
1 teaspoon ground new ginger or ⅛ teaspoon ginger powder
½ teaspoon garlic powder
½ tablespoon lemon juice
¼ cup hacked new cilantro
½ cup cleaved carrots
1 huge egg
¼ cup water
2 tablespoons canola oil

1. Put the shrimp, tofu, ginger, garlic powder, lemon juice, cilantro, carrots, egg, and water into a food processor and mix until a glue forms.

2. Scoop 2 tablespoons of glue into your hand and structure it into a stick, patty, or meatball. Rehash this progression until all of the glue is utilized up.

3. In a huge skillet, heat the oil over medium hotness. Place the shrimp sticks in the dish and fry them for 4 minutes on each side, or until they are brilliant brown.

4. Allow the shrimp sticks to cool for 5 minutes, then serve baby one stick at a time. Store extras in a sealed shut holder in the cooler for as long as 3 days. You can likewise freeze the cooked sticks on a sheet dish prior to putting away them in a water/air proof compartment to keep them from staying together. Freeze for up to 3 months.

NUT-FREE, SOY-FREE

Allergens: DAIRY, GLUTEN

MAKES 4 (½-CUP) PORTIONS | PREP TIME: 10 MINUTES | COOK TIME: 15 MINUTES

I lovethisgreenpesto pastabecauseitsneakilyincorporates vegetablesinto thesauceandisservedwithbow-tiepastaforeasy self-taking care of. Youcanusealotofdifferentkindsofgreenleafy vegetablesorherbsto createdifferentversionsofthispesto sauce. Youcanalso pairthiswithgrilledchickenor Savory Beef Meatballs foracompletemeal.

1 cup bow-tie pasta
1 cup fresh spinach
½ cup new basil
½ cup broccoli florets
¼ cup new parsley
3 garlic cloves
1 teaspoon lemon juice
½ cup olive oil
½ cup ground Parmesan cheese

1. Fill a medium pan most of the way with water and heat the water to the point of boiling over high hotness. When the water is bubbling, add the pasta and cook until it is still somewhat firm (cooked however firm), around 10 minutes. Channel the pasta.

2. While the pasta cooks, put the spinach, basil, broccoli, parsley, and garlic into a food processor and heartbeat until they are separated into more modest pieces. Add the lemon squeeze and keep on beating as you gradually pour in the oil until the pesto is smooth.

3. Heat a huge skillet over medium hotness, scratch all of the pesto into the dish, and cook until it is warmed through. Add the cooked pasta and throw to coat.

4. Let the pasta sit in the pesto sauce for 2 minutes, then, at that point, switch off the hotness and permit the pasta to cool for 5 minutes. Top with the Parmesan cheese.

5. Scoop a ½-cup segment into a bowl or plate, and let child feed themself with a fork or their hands. Guide them to eat just each necktie in turn. Store extras in an impermeable holder in the fridge for as long as 3 days or for as long as multi month in the freezer.

with deterioration. On the off chance that you get put off by the oxidized earthy colored tone, it's ideal to eat it generally that very day.

Penne Pasta with Ground Walnut Alfredo Sauce

SOY-FREE

Allergens: DAIRY, GLUTEN, NUTS

MAKES 8 (½-CUP) PORTIONS | PREP TIME: 10 MINUTES | COOK TIME: 20 MINUTES

Besidesmeltednutbutters, youcanincorporatenutsinto your baby'sdietbeforetheyturnonebysimplygrinding anyvarietyof nutsinto apowderandmixing it into differenttypesoffoods. In this formula, I'musing groundwalnutsasthey'rehighinomega-3s, whichhelpboostbraindevelopmentandhearthealth. Thisdishis goodbyitself, oryoucanpairitwithsteakorgrilledchickenand steamedbroccoli.

1 pound penne pasta
2 tablespoons unsalted
spread 1 tablespoon
universally handy flour
1 cup weighty cream or entire milk
½ cup finely ground toasted pecans
1 cup ground Parmesan cheese

1. Fill an enormous stockpot 66% brimming with water and heat the water to the point of boiling over high hotness. Pour in the pasta and cook as per the bundle guidelines until still somewhat firm, around 10 minutes. Channel the pasta and set aside.

2. While the pasta cooks, in a huge skillet, soften the margarine over medium hotness. Mix in the universally handy flour. While whisking continually, pour in the cream and keep speeding for around 8 minutes, or until the sauce is smooth with no apparent flour or lumps.

3. Stir in the ground pecans and Parmesan cheddar and cook for around brief more. Add the cooked pasta and give it a couple of throws to equitably cover the pasta with the sauce.

4. Scoop a ½-cup segment into a bowl or plate, and let child feed themself with a fork or their hands. Guide them to eat just each piece of pasta in turn. Store extras in a hermetically sealed compartment in the fridge for as long as 3 days

or for as long as multi month in the freezer.

processor, utilize that all things being equal. Attempt this with various kinds of nuts, like pistachios or almonds.

Steak and Bell Pepper Stir-Fry

CH5

12 Montths and Up

The recipes in this section continue to focus on nutrient-dense food for baby but can be used for family meals since you no longer have to portion out baby's food to cook longer, before seasoning or adding salt, and so on. At this age, baby is much more coordinated and able to use a spoon with better accuracy. However, if they still prefer using their hands and fingers, that's okay, too. Please remember that even if they are much better at eating now, you still must keep a close eye on them during mealtime. Food should be offered in strips or sticks or cut into small, cubed pieces no more than ½-inch in size.

Hemp Heart Bites

DAIRY-FREE, SOY-FREE, VEGETARIAN

Allergens: GLUTEN, NUTS

MAKES 30 BITES | PREP TIME: 15 MINUTES

Youcancertainlyofferbabyfundessertfoodsthatarealso feeding for theirbody. Theseno-bakedessertbitesarefull of flavorandnutrientsthatbabyneeds, suchasiron, fiber, and magnesium. Hempheartsalso offeralittlebitofcrunch. Youcan easilysubstitutetheoatswithgluten-freeoatsorquinoafora gluten-freedessert.

1½ cups rolled oats
½ cup hemp hearts

1 cup cleaved freeze-dried strawberries
⅔ cup salted smooth nut spread (nut, almond, or cashew)
¼ cup dim chocolate chips
2 tablespoons honey
Pinch salt (optional)

1. In an enormous bowl, combine as one the oats, hemp hearts, strawberries, nut margarine, chocolate chips, honey, and salt (if using).
2. Scoop a stacking tablespoon into your hand and structure it into a ball. Rehash this progression until all of the blend is utilized up.
3. Cut the nibbles in quarters prior to serving them to child. Store extras in a sealed shut compartment in the fridge for as long as 5 days or for as long as 90 days in the freezer.

TIP: You can likewise spread the blend on a little baking sheet in a slim layer and permit it to solidify at room temperature for around 30 minutes. Then, at that point, cut it into ½-by-4-inch strips and serve child one strip at a time.

SOY-FREE, VEGETARIAN

Allergens: DAIRY, GLUTEN, NUTS

MAKES 4 (1-CUP) PORTIONS | PREP TIME: 5 MINUTES

Smoothiesareagreatwayto adddifferentfruitsandvegetables into atoddler'sdietaswell asawayforthemto enjoytheflavorsof blendedfoods. Thissmoothiebowl is too thickforbabyto taste throughastraw. All things being equal, havethemeatitwithaspoon. Youcan topthethicksmoothiewithawidevarietyoffruitsandgrainsto maketheperfectbreakfastfood.

1½ cups frozen mixed berries (such as blackberries, blueberries, and raspberries)
½ cup full-fat plain kefir
2 cups full-fat plain or vanilla Greek yogurt
1 banana, divided
½ cup cut new strawberries, for topping
¼ cup coconut pieces, for topping
¼ cup Cheerios, for topping

1. Put the berries, kefir, yogurt, and a big part of the banana into a blender and mix until smooth, thick, and creamy.
2. Slice the other banana half into ¼-inch-thick rounds.
3. Scoop about ¾ cup of smoothie into a bowl and several cuts of banana alongside

around 1 tablespoon every one of strawberries, coconut, and Cheerios on the top.

4. Serve child the smoothie bowl with a spoon. Store the smoothie and garnishes independently in the cooler for up to 3 days.

TIP: If you have a silicone or plastic popsicle shape, fill the form with extra smoothie and stick to make ice pops. It's certain to be a hit around the house with child, more established youngsters, and adults.

DAIRY FREE, NUT-FREE, GLUTEN-FREE, SOY-FREE, VEGETARIAN
MAKES 4 (½-CUP) PORTIONS | PREP TIME: 5 MINUTES | COOK TIME: 25 MINUTES

Whenbabyisover 12 monthsold, theycanstartexploring harder leafyvegetables. Brusselssproutsareagoodoptionbecausethey holdtheirshapewell for little handsto holdonto. Rememberthat Brusselssproutshaveastrong smell, so if babydoesn'tlikethemat first, don'tbesurprised, butdon'tgiveuponoffering themto child fromtimeto time.

2 cups Brussels sprouts,
halved 1½ tablespoons olive
oil
½ teaspoon salt
⅛ teaspoon newly ground dark pepper 1
tablespoon balsamic vinegar
2 tablespoons honey

1. Preheat the broiler to 400°F.

2. Put the Brussels sprouts on an enormous baking sheet. Add the oil, salt, pepper, and vinegar and throw to cover the Brussels sprouts. Organize the Brussels sprouts on the baking sheet in an even layer.

3. Roast for around 25 minutes, or until the Brussels sprouts start to brown and to fresh at the edges.

4. Drizzle the honey over the Brussels fledglings and throw to coat.

5. Allow the Brussels sprouts to cool for 5 minutes, then cut them in half again and serve them to baby. Store extras in an impenetrable compartment in the fridge for as long as 3 days or for as long as multi month in the freezer.

DAIRY-FREE, GLUTEN-FREE, NUT-FREE, SOY-FREE, VEGETARIAN

Allergens: EGGS

MAKES 4 (½-CUP) PORTIONS | PREP TIME: 15 MINUTES | COOK TIME: 15 MINUTES

Typically, ataround a year, youcanstartexperimenting with taking care of babyfinelychoppedleafygreens-

thischoppedsaladisa goodstarting point. I useromainelettuce, asit's tenderandeasier to bite. Youcanservethissaladasanappetizerorasidewitha grainandproteindish. Sincebabyisover 12 monthsold, youcan additionally startincorporating honeyinto theirdiet.

1 large egg
1 cup finely destroyed or cleaved romaine hearts
½ cup apples, cored and cut into
matchsticks 2 tablespoons olive oil
1 tablespoon lemon juice
¼ teaspoon Dijon mustard
¼ teaspoon honey
⅛ teaspoon salt

1. Fill a little pan 66% brimming with water and heat the water to the point of boiling over medium-high hotness. Delicately slip the egg into the water and let it bubble for 10 minutes. Following 10 minutes, eliminate the egg and lower it in an ice-water shower for simple stripping. Then, removethepeelandcutthehard-boiledegg into8wedges.

2. In an enormous bowl, consolidate the romaine and apples. Add the egg wedges.

3. In a little bowl, whisk together the olive oil, lemon juice, mustard, honey, and salt and pour it over the plate of mixed greens. Prepare to uniformly cover the salad.

4. Serve a ½-cup part to child; on the off chance that you are concerned child can't bite it well, hack it into more modest pieces. Store extras in an impermeable compartment in the cooler for up to 3 days.

MAKES 6 (1-CUP) PORTIONS | PREP TIME: 10 MINUTES | COOK TIME: 20 MINUTES

Pastasaladisasimplecompletemeal thatcanbeadaptedto includeavarietyofdifferentingredientsdepending onwhattypes ofnewvegetablesyouwantyourbabyto attempt. Forthisversion, I use choppedcucumbersto introduceacrunchyvegetableasbaby continuesto mastertheirchewing skills.

1 (12-ounce) box tricolor   rotini
1 medium cucumber, cut into ½-inch dice
1 ready avocado, hollowed and cut into ½-inch
dice 1 cup cherry tomatoes, halved
1 cup Colby Jack cheddar or other hard cheddar, cut into ½-inch dice
⅔ cup Italian
dressing Salt

Freshly ground dark pepper

1. Fill a medium stockpot with water and heat the water to the point of boiling over high hotness. When the water is bubbling, add the rotini and cook until delicate, around 7 minutes. Drain the pasta and submerge it in an ice-water bath for 5 minutes, then drain it again.

2. Put the rotini in an enormous serving bowl. Add the cucumber, avocado, tomatoes, cheddar, and dressing and prepare until the pasta salad is equitably covered with dressing. Season with salt and pepper.

3. Scoop a 1-cup segment into a bowl and serve it to child with a spoon, or they can keep on utilizing their hands. Store extras in a sealed shut compartment in the fridge for up to 3 days.

NUT-FREE, SOY-FREE, VEGETARIAN

Allergens: DAIRY, GLUTEN, EGGS

MAKES 1 SANDWICH | PREP TIME: 5 MINUTES | COOK TIME: 10 MINUTES

Cheesesandwichesarethefavoritemeal ofmanyyoung youngsters. I like to addinchoppedbroccoliandturnitinto abroccolicheddar cheesesandwichforbabyto munchon. It's additionally aperfectfingerfood thatyoucanmakefortheentirefamilyforlunch.

¼ cup finely chopped broccoli
1 teaspoon water
2 cuts cheddar cheese
2 cuts entire wheat bread
1 tablespoon mayonnaise (guarantee without soy as needed)

1. Put the broccoli and water into a microwave-safe bowl and microwave it for 2 minutes. Eliminate the broccoli from the microwave and channel the water.

2. Heat a huge nonstick skillet over low hotness. Place 1 cut of cheddar on top of 1 cut of bread and top the cheddar with the broccoli. Place the second cut of cheddar on top of the broccoli and spot the second cut of bread what's more. Spread ½ tablespoon of mayonnaise outwardly top of the bread slice.

3. Place the sandwich, mayonnaise-side down, on the skillet. Spread the excess mayonnaise on the highest point of the other cut of bread. Cook for about 5 minutes, or until the bottom turns golden brown, then carefully flip the sandwich over and cook for 5 minutes more.

4. Allow the sandwich to cool for 5 minutes, then cut it into quarters or 1-inch-wide strips and serve it to baby. Assuming the external hull has become too hard and firm, trim it off prior to serving. Most babies can eat about a large portion of a sandwich in a sitting.

Chicken Tenders

NUT-FREE, SOY-FREE

Allergens: DAIRY, EGGS, GLUTEN

MAKES 12 STRIPS | PREP TIME: 10 MINUTES | COOK TIME: 15 MINUTES

Mosttoddlersenjoyeating friedfoods, andyoucaneasilyfryyour ownchickentendersathome. After 12 monthsofage, youcanstart slowlyintroducing dry, crunchytexturesto baby'sdiet. Thesehave agreatcrunch-eventhoughbabymightnothaveall oftheir molarsyet-andprovidethemwithgreatsensorystimulation.

⅓ cup all-purpose
flour 1 teaspoon salt
½ teaspoon newly ground dark pepper 2
enormous eggs
1 cup panko bread crumbs
⅔ cup ground Parmesan cheese
2 (5-to 6-ounce) boneless, skinless chicken bosoms, cut into 1½-inch-thick pieces
Oil, for cooking (around 1 cup)

1. In a little bowl, combine as one the flour, salt, and pepper.

2. In a different little bowl, beat the eggs.

3. In a medium bowl, join the bread morsels and Parmesan cheese.

4. Lightly dust one chicken delicate on all sides with the flour blend, then, at that point, plunge it into the egg combination, lastly, coat it in the breading. Rehash with the excess chicken.

5. In an enormous skillet, heat 1 inch of oil over medium hotness. When the oil begins to flicker, gradually include the chicken fingers and fry them for 6 minutes on each side, or until brilliant brown and the interior temperature arrives at 165°F.

6. Allow the tenders to cool for 5 minutes, then cut them into 3 equal strips (each about ½ inch wide) and serve baby one strip at a time. Store extras in a sealed shut holder in the fridge for as long as 3 days or for as long as multi month in the freezer.

TIP: Reheat the tenders in the broiler or on an electric barbecue. Microwaving is normally not suggested in light of the fact that the outside layer will get spongy. You can likewise begin blending the

tenders with various plunges, for example, ketchup and BBQ sauce, to permit child to investigate flavor combinations.

Tofu, Cabbage, Carrot, and Noodle Stir-Fry

DAIRY-FREE, NUT-FREE

Allergens: GLUTEN, SHELLFISH, SOY

MAKES 6 (1-CUP) PORTIONS | PREP TIME: 10 MINUTES | COOK TIME: 10 MINUTES

Thisisabalancedone-potmeal thateveryonecanenjoy. Italso introducesnewtexturesandflavorsforbabyto investigate. Youcan substituteleftovermeatforthetofuandaddorswapinother vegetablesthatyouhaveathome. Ifyoucan'tfindoystersauceor prefernotto useit, increasethesoysauceto 2 tablespoons.

1 (12-ounce) package chow mein or stir-fry noodles
2 tablespoons canola oil
1 (16-ounce) bundle firm tofu, cut into 1-inch blocks
1 tablespoon minced garlic
1 tablespoon ground new ginger
2 cups cut cabbage (½-inch-wide strips) 2
cups destroyed carrots
2 tablespoons shellfish
sauce 1 tablespoon soy
sauce
Freshly ground dark pepper

1. Fill a medium pot 66% loaded with water and heat the water to the point of boiling over medium-high hotness. When the water is bubbling, add the noodles, decrease the hotness to low, and stew for 3 minutes. Channel and set aside.

2. While the noodles cook, in an enormous skillet, heat the oil over medium hotness. Add the tofu and fry for around 3 minutes on each side, or until brilliant brown. Eliminate the tofu from the container and set aside.

3. Put the garlic and ginger into a similar skillet and sautéed food until fragrant, around 1 moment. Add the cabbage and carrots and keep on blending until the cabbage begins to shrivel, around 2 minutes. Return the tofu to the skillet and add the noodles, clam sauce, and soy sauce. Keep cooking and mixing until everything is all around blended, around 2 minutes. Season with dark pepper to taste.

4. Scoop a ½-cup segment into a bowl and permit it to cool for 3 minutes prior to serving it to

child. On the off chance that you are restless with regards to the long noodles, cut them into 5-inch lengths. Store extras in a sealed shut holder in the fridge for as long as 3 days or for as long as multi month in the freezer.

DAIRY-FREE, GLUTEN-FREE, NUT-FREE, VEGETARIAN

Allergens: EGGS, SOY

MAKES 4 (1-CUP) PORTIONS | PREP TIME: 5 MINUTES | COOK TIME: 10 MINUTES

Thisisthego-to dinner forourfamilyonceaweekwhenweclearout all theleftoverfoodinourrefrigerator. Youcanuseleftover Chicken Tenders, Pork Chops, oreven Salmon Patties tomixinat theend. Ifyourbabyisstill under 18 monthsold, it is bestto chopthe edamameinto smallerpieces(aboutpeasize).

**1 large egg, beaten
2 cups cooked white rice (ideally chilled/extra rice) 3
tablespoons olive oil
1 cup frozen edamame, defrosted and cleaved
1 cup frozen peas and carrots
½ teaspoon salt
½ teaspoon newly ground dark pepper**

1. Heat a huge nonstick or cast-iron skillet over medium heat.
2. In a medium bowl, mix the egg into the rice until the egg covers the rice grains.
3. Once the dish is hot, add the oil and hotness it until it shimmers. Add the rice and spread it out equally in the dish. Increase the heat to medium-high and let the rice cook for 3 minutes, then start stirring frequently to sauté the rice.
4. Stir in the edamame, peas and carrots, salt, and pepper. Mix to blend the vegetables equitably into the rice. Keep cooking and blending once each moment to turn the rice and vegetable combination until the vegetables are warmed through, around 5 minutes.
5. Scoop a ½-to 1-cup segment into a bowl and let it cool for 5 minutes prior to serving it to child. Urge child to work on eating it with a spoon. Store extras in a hermetically sealed holder in the cooler for 3 days or for as long as multi month in the freezer.

GLUTEN-FREE, NUT-FREE, SOY-FREE

Allergens: DAIRY

SERVES 4 | PREP TIME: 5 MINUTES | COOK TIME: 20 MINUTES

Porkchopscaneasilybeovercookedandbecomedryandtough, so I like to cooktheminalittlebitofbrothto retainmoistureanduse applecidervinegar, orotheracid, to keepthemtenderandjuicy.

2 **tablespoons olive oil**
1 **tablespoon salted butter**
4 **(1-inch-thick) boneless pork chops**
¼ **teaspoon salt**
¼ **teaspoon newly ground dark pepper**
¼ **cup apple juice vinegar**
¼ **cup low-sodium vegetable or chicken broth**
2 **tablespoons slashed new rosemary or 2 teaspoons dried rosemary**
2 **medium apples, cored and each cut into 8 wedges**

1. In a huge skillet, heat the oil over medium-high hotness, then, at that point, add the butter.

2. Season every pork cleave with salt and pepper, then, at that point, put them in the skillet, ensuring that they are equally divided. Singe for 5 minutes on each side, or until the meat starts to brown.

3. Reduce the hotness to medium and pour in the apple juice vinegar and stock. Orchestrate the rosemary and apples in the middle of the pork cleaves. Cover and let stew for around 5 minutes, or until the pork hacks are cooked through and the inward temperature arrives at 145°F.

4. Allow the pork chops to cool for 5 minutes, then cut one into ½-inch-wide strips (or smaller pieces) and serve baby the strips one at a time. Store extras in an impenetrable holder in the cooler for as long as 3 days or for as long as multi month in the freezer.

MAKES 5 (1-CUP) PORTIONS | PREP TIME: 10 MINUTES | COOK TIME: 15 MINUTES

Couscousisasemolinapastathatisagoodsourceofproteinand likewise selenium, akeymineral forbrainandimmunesystemhealth. I like to rotatedifferenttypesofgrainsinto thefamilymeal for varietyandto letbabyexperiencenewtextures. Ifyouarea vegetarianfamily, simplyomitthechickenandaddwhatever plant-basedproteinyouwish. Ifyouhaveleftovervegetables, you canusethoseupinthisrecipe.

2 **(5-ounce) boneless, skinless chicken breasts, cut into 1-inch cubes**
½ **teaspoon salt**
¼ **teaspoon newly ground dark pepper**
½ **teaspoon garlic powder**
⅛ **teaspoon ground**

cumin 2 tablespoons
olive oil
1 cup hacked cauliflower florets
1 cup cherry tomatoes, halved
½ cup frozen peas
1 cup couscous
10 ounces low-sodium chicken or vegetable broth
¼ cup slashed new parsley

1. Season the chicken with the salt, pepper, garlic powder, and cumin.

2. In a huge skillet, heat the oil over medium hotness. Add the chicken and cook it for 3 minutes on each side. Add the cauliflower, tomatoes, and peas and keep cooking and mixing for around 3 minutes. Add the couscous and blend well.

3. Pour in the stock and heat it to the point of boiling. When it's bubbling, decrease the hotness to low, cover, and stew for 7 minutes, or until the couscous is feathery and delicate. Decorate with the parsley.

4. Scoop a ½-to 1-cup segment into a bowl and permit it to cool for 5 minutes prior to serving it to child. Urge child to work on utilizing a spoon, or they can involve their hands for greater things, like the chicken and vegetables. Store extras in a sealed shut compartment in the fridge for as long as 3 days or for as long as multi month in the freezer.

Mini Turkey Burgers

NUT-FREE, SOY-FREE

Allergens: DAIRY, EGGS, GLUTEN

MAKES 6 MINI BURGERS | PREP TIME: 10 MINUTES | COOK TIME: 15 MINUTES

Burgersareafuncombinationfoodto introduceto child, andyou canmixtheturkeywithdifferenttypesofvegetablesto makeit morenutritiousandeasierto handle. Youmayfindthatsome babiesdon'tliketheirdifferentfoodstouching, butthat'sokay-you canservetheburgerdeconstructed.

8 ounces 90% lean ground turkey
¼ teaspoon salt
⅛ teaspoon newly ground dark pepper
½ teaspoon garlic powder
½ teaspoon onion powder
½ teaspoon paprika
⅔ cup finely cleaved broccoli or vegetables of choice
⅔ cup finely hacked button mushrooms

½ **cup destroyed cheddar 2**
tablespoons canola oil
6 party rolls or Hawaiian sweet rolls

1. In an enormous bowl, combine as one the turkey, salt, pepper, garlic powder, onion powder, paprika, broccoli, mushrooms, and cheddar until well combined.

2. Scoop 2 storing tablespoons of the turkey combination into your hand and structure it into a patty. Place the patty on a plate. Rehash with the excess turkey mixture.

3. In a huge nonstick skillet, heat the oil over medium hotness. Organize the patties in the skillet and cook them for around 5 minutes on each side, or until they are brilliant brown and the inner temperature arrives at 165°F.

4. While the patties are cooking, split the rolls and daintily toast them on an iron or in a toaster oven oven.

5. Place the patties on the rolls. Slice one down the middle or more modest (no more extensive than 1 inch) and permit it to cool for 5 minutes prior to serving it to child. Store extra patties in a water/air proof compartment in the cooler for as long as 3 days or for as long as multi month in the freezer.

TIP: Make sure to delicately toast the rolls you use in light of the fact that untoasted bread will in general shape a tacky, pale surface at the rear of the throat and may cause choking or potential choking.

Steak and Bell Pepper Stir-Fry

GLUTEN-FREE, NUT-FREE, SOY-FREE

Allergens: DAIRY

MAKES 6 (½-CUP) PORTIONS | PREP TIME: 10 MINUTES | COOK TIME: 15 MINUTES

Ataround 12 monthsofage, babieswithteethwill beableto chomp throughthetoughertextureofmeat. Buteveniftheycan't, sucking andgnawing onsteakwill still offergoodnutritionastheycan extractironfromthemeat'sjuices. Servebabywell-donesteakto avoidtheriskoffoodpoisoning. Remindthemto takesmallerbites andchewwell. Useatendercutofmeat, suchastheoptionslisted beneath, to makesureitiseasierforbabyto chew.

1 pound steak (petite sirloin, sirloin, or petite shoulder), cut into 1-by-4-inch strips
¼ cup plain unsweetened yogurt
3 tablespoons olive oil, divided
1 green chime pepper, cultivated and cut into ½-inch-wide

**strips 1 red ringer pepper, cultivated and cut into ½-inch-
wide strips
¼ cup steak sauce
Freshly ground dark pepper
Salt**

1. In a medium bowl or zip-top pack, consolidate the meat and the yogurt and permit the meat to marinate for 10 minutes on the ledge. The corrosive in the yogurt will help soften the meat.
2. While the meat marinates, in a huge skillet, heat 1 tablespoon of oil over medium hotness. Add the green and red ringer peppers and sauté for 3 minutes, mixing much of the time. Move the ringer peppers to a plate.
3. Put the leftover 2 tablespoons of oil into the skillet and increment the hotness to medium-high. Place the steak strips in the dish and burn them for around 3 minutes on each side.
4. Stir in the steak sauce, until the meat is well coated, then return the bell peppers to the pan and continue cooking and stirring for another 2 minutes, or until the steak is cooked through and the internal temperature reaches 160°F. Season with dark pepper and salt to taste.
5. Allow the steak to cool for 5 minutes, then serve baby one strip at a time, or cut the strips into smaller pieces. Store extras in an impermeable holder in the fridge for as long as 3 days or for as long as multi month in the freezer.

TIP: You can likewise allow your child to chew on one segment of steak with one hand and proposition a few cut-up pieces, as well. There are no severe guidelines; it depends on your child's formative capacity and your solace level.

Volume Equivalents	U.S. STANDARD	U.S. STANDARD (OUNCES)	METRIC (APPROXIMATE)
Liquid	2 tablespoons	1 fl. oz.	30 mL
	¼ cup	2 fl. oz.	60 mL
	½ cup	4 fl. oz.	120 mL
	1 cup	8 fl. oz.	240 mL
	1½ cups	12 fl. oz.	355 mL
	2 cups or 1 pint	16 fl. oz.	475 mL
	4 cups or 1 quart	32 fl. oz.	1 L
	1 gallon	128 fl. oz.	4 L
Dry	⅛ teaspoon	—	0.5 mL
	¼ teaspoon	—	1 mL
	½ teaspoon	—	2 mL
	¾ teaspoon	—	4 mL
	1 teaspoon	—	5 mL
	1 tablespoon	—	15 mL
	¼ cup	—	59 mL
	⅓ cup	—	79 mL
	½ cup	—	118 mL
	⅔ cup	—	156 mL
	¾ cup	—	177 mL
	1 cup	—	235 mL
	2 cups or 1 pint	—	475 mL
	3 cups	—	700 mL
	4 cups or 1 quart	—	1 L
	½ gallon	—	2 L
	1 gallon	—	4 L

Oven Temperatures		Weight Equivalents	
FAHRENHEIT	CELSIUS (APPROXIMATE)	U.S. STANDARD	METRIC (APPROXIMATE)
250°F	120°C	½ ounce	15 g
300°F	150°C	1 ounce	30 g
325°F	165°C	2 ounces	60 g
350°F	180°C	4 ounces	115 g
375°F	190°C	8 ounces	225 g
400°F	200°C	12 ounces	340 g
425°F	220°C	16 ounces or	455 g
450°F	230°C	1 pound	

These are a couple of extra assets that guardians can allude to and more deeply study child's taking care of excursion and child drove weaning.

Baby-Led Weaning: Helping Your Babyto Love Good Food by Gill Rapley and Tracey Murkett (London: Random House UK, 2009)

Ellyn Satter Institute, EllynSatterInstitute.org/family-meals-focus/78-baby-led-weaning

Signing Time Dictionary: Mealtime, SigningTime.com/word reference/classification/mealtime

Solid Starts, SolidStarts.com

American Academy of Allergy, Asthma, and Immunology. "Prevention of Allergies and Asthma in Children." September 28, 2020. AAAAI.org/Tools-for-the-Public/Conditions-Library/Allergies/prevention-of-allergies-and-asthma-in-children.

American Academy of Pediatrics. "Beginning Solid Foods." Last updated March 17, 2021. HealthyChildren.org/English/ages-stages/child/taking care of nourishment/Pages/Starting-Solid-Foods.aspx.

American Red Cross. "Cognizant Choking: Cannot Cough, Speak, Cry or Breathe." RedCross.org/content/dam/redcross/atg/PDF_s/ConsciousCho

Brown, Amy, Sara Wyn Jones, and Hannah Rowan. "Child Led Weaning: The Evidence to Date." Current Nutrition Reports 6, no. 2 (2017): 148-56. doi.org/10.1007/s13668-017-0201-2.

Daniels, Lisa, Anne-Louise M. Heath, Sheila M. Williams, Sonya L. Cameron, Elizabeth A. Fleming, Barry J. Taylor, Rosalind S. Gibson, and Rachael W. Taylor. "Child Led Introduction to Solids (BLISS) Study: A Randomized Controlled Trial of a Baby-Led Approach to Complementary Feeding." BMCPediatrics 15, no. 179 (2015). doi.org/10.1186/s12887-015-0491-8.

Du Toit George, Graham Roberts, Peter H. Sayre, Henry T. Bahnson, Suzana Radulovic, Alexandra F. Santos, Helen A. Brough, et al. "Randomized Trial of Peanut Consumption in Infants at Risk for Peanut Allergy." New England Journal of Medicine 372, no. 9 (2015): 803-13. doi.org/10.1056/NEJMoa1414850.

Fangupo, Louise J., Anne-Louise M. Heath, Sheila M. Williams, Liz W. Erickson Williams, Brittany J. Morison, Elizabeth A. Fleming, Barry J. Taylor, Benjamin J. Wheeler, and Rachael W. Taylor. "A Baby-Led Approach to Eating Solids and Risk of Choking." Pediatrics 138, no. 4 (2016). doi.org/10.1542/peds.2016-0772.

Fleischer, David M., Jonathan M. Spergel, Amal H. Assa'ad, and Jacqueline A. Pongracic. "Essential Prevention of Allergic Disease through Nutritional Interventions." Journal of Allergyand Clinical Immunology: *In Practice 1*, no. 1 (2013): 29-36. doi.org/10.1016/j.jaip.2012.09.003.

Greer, FrAnk R., Scott H. Sicherer, A. Wesley Burks, American Academy of Pediatrics Committee on Nutrition, American Academy of Pediatrics Section on Allergy and Immunology. "The Effects of Early Nutritional Interventions on the Development of Atopic Disease in Infants and Children: The Role of Maternal Dietary Restriction, Breastfeeding, Timing of Introduction of Complementary Foods, and Hydrolyzed Formulas." Pediatrics 121, no. 1 (2008): 183-91. doi.org/10.1542/peds.2007-3022.

Haase, F. Robert, and Arnold Brenner. "Esophageal Diameters at Various Ages." Archivesof Otolaryngology 77, no.2 (1963): 15-18. doi.org/10.1001/archotol.77.2.15.

Mayo Clinic Staff. "Gagging: First Aid." MayoClinic.org/medical aid/emergency treatment stifling/rudiments/craftsmanship 20056637.